Composers of the Low Countries

Composers of the Low Countries

WILLEM ELDERS

Translated by
GRAHAM DIXON

Clarendon Press · Oxford

1991

Oxford University Press, Walton Street, Oxford OX2 6DP
Oxford   New York   Toronto
Delhi   Bombay   Calcutta   Madras   Karachi
Petaling Jaya   Singapore   Hong Kong   Tokyo
Nairobi   Dar es Salaam   Cape Town
Melbourne   Auckland
and associated companies in
Berlin   Ibadan

Oxford is a trade mark of Oxford University Press

Published in the United States
by Oxford University Press, New York

First published in 1985 by Bohn, Scheltema & Holkema BV, Utrecht
First published in English in 1990 by Oxford University Press

British Library Cataloguing in Publication Data
Elders, Willem
Composers of the low countries.
1. Music of Benelux. Composers
I. Title   II. Componisten van de lage landen. English
780'.92'2
ISBN 0-19-816147-6

Library of Congress Cataloging in Publication Data
Composers of the Low Countries / Willem Elders;
translated by Graham Dixon.
Translation of: Componisten van de Lage Landen.
Includes bibliographical references.
1. Music—Netherlands—History and criticism—15th century.
2. Music—Netherlands—History and criticism—16th century.
I. Title.
ML265.2.E4413   1990   780'.9492'09024—dc20   89-70829
ISBN 0-19-816147-6

Printed in Great Britain by
Biddles Ltd., Guildford and King's Lynn

In memory of
David Munrow

PREFACE

In 1506 the Venetian ambassador to Flanders, Vincenzo Quirini, reported to his government as follows: 'In detto paese tre cose sono di somma eccellenzza: tele sottilissime e belle in copia in Olanda; tapezzerie bellissime in figure in Brabante; la terza è la musica, la quale certamente si puo dire che sia perfetta.'[1] (In this country there are three things of the highest quality; the fine, beautiful linen from Holland; the most beautiful tapestries from Brabant; and the third is music, which one may certainly say is perfect.) The reader of these lines might well ask himself why the ambassador did not mention painting. Were not the Southern Netherlands at that time the cradle of the unsurpassed art of the Flemish Primitives?

Interest in the work of Jan van Eyck, Hans Memling, Rogier van der Weyden, and Jeroen Bosch, to name only a few, can be taken completely for granted. We are still enthralled by the achievements of these painters, as were, for example, Philip the Good, Nicolas Rolin of Beaune, and Philip the Fair, who honoured them with great commissions. But even if the question posed above cannot be answered with certainty, the music historian may understand that Quirini was impressed by the music that he could hear at the court of Margaret of Austria in Malines, in the Church of Our Lady in Antwerp, and in many other places in the Netherlands. Venice in his time was still only at the very beginning of its own musical development. It was a Fleming who from about 1530, as *maestro di cappella* of St Mark's Basilica, laid the ground for a school of composers, who made Venice a renowned centre for lovers of music. The changes which took place in Quirini's home city could also be witnessed almost throughout Europe. From Munich, Prague, and Budapest to Madrid, Milan, and Naples musicians from the Netherlands were in demand in order to contribute to the daily musical activity in courts and churches.

Though streets in various Dutch and Belgian towns are named after composers of the fifteenth and the sixteenth centuries, those who bore these names have, in the eyes of many, remained unknown masters. Who was Johannes Ockeghem, for whom no less than Erasmus wrote an elegy?

---

[1] *Relazioni degli ambasciatori veneti al Senato,* ed. A. Albéri, ser. 1, pt. 1 (Florence, 1839), 11f.

F I G. I. Portrait of Orlando di Lasso at the age of forty, painted by Hans Mielich. The composer is dressed in his gown and holds a glove in his left hand, a sign of nobility, and in the right hand a roll of music paper. The miniature is found on the last page of the magnificent codex containing penitential psalms (Part II), which Albrecht V of Bavaria commissioned for his court in 1563–70 (see also Fig. 7). Munich, Bayerische Staatsbibliothek, Mus. Ms. A.

Who was Josquin, whom Luther so much admired? Who was Orlando di Lasso, who was showered with honours by pope and king (see Fig. 1)? This book seeks to answer these questions. The music of the Netherlands composers is its central topic, but this will be described in the context of the culture of which it formed a part. Thus we shall examine the background from which these composers approached musical composition. A study of connections between the musical structure of a composition and the text on which it is based may explain why these musicians were so celebrated in their time.

Obviously considerable attention should be given to sacred music. In the late Middle Ages and the Renaissance Christian thought occupied a central place in people's lives. But the secular element also played a large role. A passing look through this book shows that many Netherlands composers knew the French as well as the Italian or German language. Through their musical settings they gave an extra dimension to the most beautiful contemporary Western poetry; Petrarch, Ronsard, Christine de Pisan, and Jean Molinet appealed more to the ears than to the eyes. And it is above all in music that the explanation for this must be sought.

Moreover, I have tried to say something about the position which the composer occupied in society; in many cases his choir robes symbolized only a part of his talents. Finally, there are short biographical sketches of fifty composers, intended to provide a quicker orientation in the world of Netherlands early music. A large number of technical terms are explained in the Glossary. Biblical passages are quoted from the Jerusalem Bible.

This book owes its origin to a generation of interested and challenging students at Utrecht University, with whom I have shared ideas over the years. I also learned much from several colleagues and other experts, of whom Dr Rebecca Stewart should be mentioned in particular.

W.E.

Tull en 't Waal
New Year 1985

In addition to my thanks to Graham Dixon for his translation I am indebted to Dr Willem Adriaansz for his valuable assistance in reading Dr Dixon's work. I am grateful too for Fiona Little's painstaking and exemplary editorial work.

W.E.

Tull en 't Waal
1989

CONTENTS

1
Introduction

DID A NETHERLANDS SCHOOL EVER EXIST?

IN contemporary writing about music the term 'Netherlands School' is generally accepted, but it is striking that authors never or rarely justify the use of the term. Because this attitude on the part of writers may be the result either of a musical situation which speaks for itself or of a faulty historical perspective, it seems reasonable to examine if, or to what extent, conclusive arguments for the use of this term were formulated in the past.

The term 'Netherlanders' was employed several times in music historiography before the first study specifically dedicated to the 'Netherlands School' appeared. Thus Charles Burney corrects a statement concerning Ockeghem's origins in his *General History of Music* (1776): according to him Johannes Ockeghem was referred to by his contemporaries as if he were a 'Netherlander'. John Hawkins, writing in his *General History of the Science and Practice of Music* (also published in 1776), states that Jacob Obrecht was a 'Fleming' and that Ockeghem came from the 'Low Countries'. Johann Forkel in his *Allgemeine Geschichte der Musik* of 1801 says of Obrecht that he was 'one of the earliest contrapuntists among the Netherlanders'.

The year 1826 is of great importance for this problem, since in that year Kiesewetter's study *Die Verdienste der Niederländer um die Tonkunst* appeared. Here, for the first time, it is explicitly stated that the 'Netherlanders' constituted a school—to be precise Kiesewetter speaks of three schools in succession—because a specific technique was used by a particular group of composers, namely invertible counterpoint. The word 'school' is employed by this author to mean teachers and pupils working in the same style.

It is worth noting that, according to Kiesewetter, all composers from Germany, France, Spain, and Italy 'who flourished until the end of the sixteenth century', and who imitated the Netherlands technique of invertible counterpoint, should be counted among the 'Netherlands School'. Even if musicology no longer shares this opinion, Kiesewetter's term 'Netherlands School' has become common property. The music historian has apparently established, or supposes, that the composers nowadays called 'Netherlanders' had something in common.

Given the enormous stylistic and structural diversity within the repertoire of the so-called Netherlands School and the impact that this music had on other repertoires, the assumption that such a common element should be sought in the music itself seems hardly justified. Moreover, if one applies geographical criteria—associating potential Netherlands composers with a Netherlands motherland—one soon encounters the problem that the origins of many composers are unknown, as well as the places where they worked.

It appears then that the term 'Netherlands School' can be justifiably used only to refer to the group of composers for whom there is evidence of proven Netherlands descent, or who were part of a known teacher–pupil relationship which led to common stylistic traits.

THE NETHERLANDS IN THE FIFTEENTH AND SIXTEENTH CENTURIES

The term 'Low Countries' figures in the title of this book. It is well known that this embraces the 'low lands by the sea', or 'Netherlands', those areas of Western Europe which, during the fifteenth and sixteenth centuries, were united in a certain dynastic relationship by the dukes of Burgundy and later by Charles V. Originally the term 'Netherlands' was used only occasionally, but in the sixteenth century it became increasingly common to speak of 'Les pays de par deçà', the 'lands beyond', or 'Les Pays-Bas'. From about 1550 onwards the term 'Netherlands' appears in official documents.

The regions which belonged to the Burgundian Netherlands before 1500 included Holland, Zeeland, Brabant, Flanders, Artois, Hainault, and Luxemburg. In the sixteenth century Charles V added Utrecht and the northeastern provinces to his possessions. Liège remained independent under the control of a prince-bishop. Though the Burgundians made conscious efforts to bring about a certain political unity, these regions never became a permanent state. Following the Netherlands rebellion at the end of the sixteenth century an independent republic came into being in the north, while the southern provinces (roughly present-day Belgium) remained under Spanish rule, and later under that of the Austrian Habsburgs. Moreover, in the seventeenth century Artois and parts of Flanders and Hainault were annexed by France. The Duchy of Burgundy itself had already fallen into French hands in 1477.

The Netherlands in the fifteenth and sixteenth centuries constituted only a very weak political entity, and it was also rather divided in other respects; for instance, at least three languages were spoken there. None the less, in the musical field there was a certain unity. One explanation for this lay in its ecclesiastical organization: the three dioceses of Tournai, Cambrai, and Liège covered an area that included present-day Belgium and Dutch Brabant; in the east it extended to Aachen. Because of the sophisticated urban life and the high level of prosperity in this region, compared with the rest of Europe at that time—only northern Italy could compete with the Netherlands—musical talent was offered every opportunity to develop to the full. The cathedral choir schools of Liège, Cambrai, Antwerp, Bruges, and 's-Hertogenbosch played a particularly important role in this.

THE STATE OF MUSIC IN WESTERN EUROPE ABOUT 1400

The political situation in the Low Countries meant that this region came under the influence of French culture during the rule of the Burgundian dukes. There were numerous French-speaking state officials in Flanders and Brabant, and the dukes were generally accompanied by artists from the Burgundian court even during their frequent journeys to the north. Even today, the extent to which there was a separate tradition of Netherlands polyphonic music during the fourteenth century is not known. Nevertheless, about 1400 the first composers of the Netherlands School sought their point of departure in the existing French compositional techniques.

Philippe de Vitry (d 1361) and Guillaume de Machaut (d 1377) may be regarded as the most important composers of the so-called *Ars nova* period. The most common musical form of this period is the motet. The subject-matter of this genre is amorous, political, or social. French and Latin texts appear simultaneously, and the musical structure commonly shows complicated isoperiodic patterns (see p. 32). Besides the motet there is French discant song, which consists of a sung upper part, and one to three accompanying instrumental parts; the most common poetic forms are the ballade, rondeau, and virelai. On the death of Machaut no essential changes occurred, yet rhythm was refined to its limits; in this context one speaks of the *Ars subtilior*. Tapissier, Carmen, and Cesaris belonged to the new generation of composers. They shared the Christian name Johannes, and all three were mentioned as representatives of a melodious art of song composition by Martin le Franc in his *Champion des dames*.

However, one should not leap to the conclusion that the Netherlanders modelled their own music exclusively on the musical means of expression used by their southern colleagues. The assimilation of the polyphonic interplay of melodic lines, which was based mainly on learned structural principles, went together with the search for more pleasing harmony and a melodic line which followed the text more closely.

It was unquestionably because of the Hundred Years War that the Continent came under the influence of English music. Manuscripts preserved in Cambrai, Paris, Munich, Vienna, Trent, Aosta, and Modena witness to the presence of English musicians. The greatest of these, John Dunstable (*d* 1453), lived for years in France in the retinue of the Duke of Bedford, the commander of the English armies. Dunstable's epitaph names him as the 'confederate of the stars'. He was indeed recognized as one of the most famed astronomers of his time, and in this capacity he undoubtedly assisted the duke in his military undertakings.

When Martin le Franc wrote his *Champion des dames* for Philip the Good at the beginning of the 1440s, he also dedicated a song to the state of French art. One of the six couplets concerned with music reads as follows:

> Car ilz ont nouvelle pratique
> De faire frisque concordance
> En haulte et en basse musique,
> En fainte, en pause et en muance,
> Et ont prins de la contenance
> Angloise et ensuivy Dunstable
> Pourquoy merveilleuse plaissance
> Rend leur chant joyeulx et notable.[1]

> For they have a new practice
> Of making fresh concordance
> In loud and soft music
> With *ficta*, pauses, and mutations.
> In this they follow the guise
> Of the English and Dunstable,
> Their song sounds wonderfully pleasant,
> So joyous and so notable.

---

[1] Royal Library, Brussels, Ms. 9466, fo. 120[r v]. The complete passage may be found in the brochure of the Dufay Commemoration, the Festival van Vlaanderen (Louvain, 1974), 80.

'Ilz' refers to Guillaume Dufay and Gilles Binchois, two of the first great Netherlands composers, and by 'contenance angloise' Le Franc meant the harmonies used in England, which were sweeter than those of the Continent due to the many thirds and sixths. Also, many so-called block chords and consonant chordal progressions were used in England.[2] The focus here lay in sacred music: the setting of sections of the Mass Ordinary (Gloria, Credo, Sanctus, and Agnus Dei) was of particular significance, because in these a cyclic musical cohesion was brought about for the first time.

The Netherlanders adopted elements of Italian music as well as of French and English. In a period when writers such as Dante, Petrarch, and Boccaccio contributed fundamentally to the development of Italian as a poetic language, composers, influenced by the expanding literary humanism, were bound to strive towards a faithful musical presentation of the text. This meant that the important words and long syllables were set with more appropriate musical expression than was usual elsewhere. For instance, the famous Florentine poet-musician Francesco Landini (*d* 1397) and some of his contemporaries wrote madrigals in which the shape of the music was affected in a detailed way by the content of the text.

With this music as a model, the first Netherlanders who left for Italy, such as Johannes Ciconia, Arnold de Lantins, and Dufay, sought to arrive at a synthesis between French polyphony, English harmony, and Italian text-setting. One can learn how fruitful this amalgamation of diverse national elements was for the development of music by studying the history of the Netherlands School.

Meanwhile we must consider the question of how musical activity was developing in Germany and Spain. Though the practice of music flourished in these countries too, until about 1450 they remained completely in the background as regards the development of polyphony. Certainly some Spanish medieval sources containing polyphonic motets, organa, and sequences are known. Yet this music, found chiefly along the pilgrim route to Santiago de Compostela, owes a great deal to the French polyphonic art. The following paragraphs will outline the stimulating effect that the arrival of Netherlands musicians had on the music of this part of Western Europe.

---

[2] The use of this harmony, progressive for its time, may indicate that England played a greater role in the development of polyphony than is generally acknowledged. The well-known rota *Sumer is icumen in*, the earliest ever piece of six-part polyphony, was composed as early as *c.*1250.

THE MIGRATION OF NETHERLANDERS TO CENTRAL AND SOUTHERN EUROPE

One of the most noteworthy aspects of Renaissance musical life is probably its cosmopolitan nature. In fact, this phenomenon is not only noteworthy, but also extremely important. To make an analogy, when we admire the stylistic diversity in the music of J. S. Bach, we must realize that this is the result of a synthesis that Bach made of the German, Italian, and French styles. A similar development came about in the Netherlands School some two or three centuries earlier as a result of the Netherlanders residing in other European countries and the consequent interaction between their style and that of the native composers.

Archival research has shown that singers from the Netherlands worked in almost all European states during the Renaissance. Most of their names have been forgotten. However, those who were also active as composers commonly enjoyed splendid careers, and some of them even gained international fame during their lifetimes. One might ask why this emigration of talented musicians took place.

There is no definite answer to this question. But it seems quite certain that the explanation is not to be found in a saturation of the employment market in the Netherlands. It was chiefly the most prominent Netherlanders who journeyed widely and remained abroad for many years, sometimes for the greatest part of their lives. It is scarcely imaginable that there would have been no attractive positions for them in the rich regions of Flanders, Brabant, Hainault, or Burgundy. These musicians must also have known that nowhere else in Europe had music reached such a high level as in their own homeland. Was it perhaps the brilliant Italian Renaissance culture that awakened the desire to travel in the first *oltremontani*?

In this connection it is worth remembering that not only musicians went south, but also artists and students. Undoubtedly, the highly developed court culture and university institutions in Italy strongly attracted the northerners. And naturally, many artists and musicians were directly recruited by popes and cardinals, emperors and kings, dukes and noble families. Among these music-loving patrons one could name Eugenius IV and Leo X; the Malatesta of Rimini, the Estensi of Ferrara, the Sforza of Milan, and the Medici of Florence; Charles VII of France, Isabella of Castille, Ferdinando I of Naples, Mathias Corvinus of Hungary, and Sigismund I of Poland; Albrecht V and Wilhelm V of Bavaria; Maximilian I, Philip the Fair, Charles V, and Maximilian II.

FIG 2. The theorist Adrianus Petit Coclico as he appears in his *Compendium musices* (Nuremberg, 1552). Coclico is one of the few Netherlanders who emigrated to Germany (see also Fig. 22). The words of the canon, 'Desperate I hope', also appear at the end of a letter from Coclico to Duke Albrecht of Prussia, in which the composer states that he will send him a copy of his *Compendium*, and in which he recommends himself to the favour of the duke.

However important the role which patronage exercised in explaining the emigration of the Netherlanders, some element of chance certainly played a part on occasions. The possession of a beautiful voice could in itself have provided the motive, as in the case of Orlando di Lasso from Mons in Hainault. As a child he was apparently abducted three times, and at the age of 13 he had already arrived in Palermo by way of Mantua.[3] Chance also seems to have had some effect on the career of the first Netherlands composer who is known for certain to have resided in Italy, Ciconia of Liège. By way of the papal court in Avignon he appears to have visited several Italian cities in the service of the Spanish Peace Ambassador Cardinal Albornoz. Shortly after 1400 he settled in Padua, where he died in 1411. Philippus de Monte must be mentioned as one of the last Netherlanders to have made a career outside his country. The following picture emerges from some glimpses at the life of this musician from Malines: in 1542 the 21-year-old composer was in the service of a Neapolitan family; in 1554 he stayed in England for a short while as a member of the private chapel of Philip II after his marriage to Mary Tudor in 1553; from 1 May 1568 he was Kapellmeister at the Habsburg court, successively under Maximilian II and Rudolf II: in this capacity he resided in Vienna and Prague, and he died in the latter city in 1603.

On the basis of this sketch of the political and social situation we can understand why the composers from the Low Countries often bore names which are, in fact, neither Dutch nor French. It is obvious that a surname such as Chywogne would have been altered to 'Ciconia' in Italy, and that Johannes Wreede would have been called 'Johannes Ur(r)ede' in Spain. When moreover a name admits translation, a colourful assortment of variants may evolve.[4] Pierre de la Rue is recorded in Latin treatises as 'Petrus Platensis' or 'de Platea'; this composer gives us the only example of a name being translated into Dutch, as 'Peteren van Straten'. Josquin des Prez was also alloted Latin and Italian names: 'Jusquinus', 'Jodocus Pratensis' (or 'de Prato'), and 'Juschino'. In contrast with La Rue's name there seems to have been no mention of a Dutch equivalent: the form 'Jooske van de Weiden', sometimes used in modern writings, is never found in old sources. But Latin and Italian names do not always prove to be 'translations'. Until recently it was thought that Cypriano de Rore came from Malines,[5] and it was therefore sometimes suggested that his name

---

[3] See H. Leuchtmann, *Orlando di Lasso. Sein Leben* (Wiesbaden, 1976), 81 f.

[4] I myself experienced the speed with which Italians proceed to translate foreign names when I was in Italy in 1960. Some friends instantly named me 'Guglielmo Altrove'.

[5] Even in the renowned *New Grove Dictionary of Music and Musicians* (London, 1980), Malines is still referred to as the birthplace of Rore.

was a Latin version of 'Van den Dauwe'. It has now been shown that this composer must have been born in Ronse, a town where many Rores (Roderes) lived. There is even a graffito in the crypt of St Hermes's Church in Ronse in which the name 'Rore' appears together with the family coat of arms showing two crossed scythes, the same as that on the composer's gravestone in Parma.[6]

The signature of Philippe de Monte

CENTRES OF MUSIC

It is clear from the discussion above that the centres where music of the Netherlands School flourished are not to be sought exclusively in the Low Countries. However, this section will be restricted to naming a number of towns in the Netherlands itself. For details of other centres the reader is referred to the biographical summaries of composers in the Appendix.

Our knowledge of the history of musical life in the fifteenth and sixteenth centuries is based in large measure on archival data. In towns where these are missing, incomplete, or not yet researched, one can only conjecture about musical life. Even where the church and town archives have been studied it is seldom possible to give a full account. Too often the contemporary chronicler only wrote about the social aspect of musical activity or limited himself to insubstantial marginal notes; and frequently it was only the salaries that were deemed important enough to note in writing.

Working from north to south, the first place worthy of mention is Amsterdam, where Sweelinck lived. The well-known pilgrimage chapel, the 'Heilige Stede' or the Nieuwezijdskapel, received a beautiful illuminated choirbook for use on Corpus Christi from the Amsterdam banker

---

[6] See A. Cambier, 'De grootste roem van de stad Ronse: de komponist Cypriaan de Ro(de)re, "omnium musicorum princeps"', *Annalen Geschied- en Oudheidkundige Kring van Ronse en het Tenement van Inde*, 30 (1981), 5–56; and idem, 'De definitieve bevestiging van Cypriaan De Rore's Ronsische afkomst uit archiefstukken te Parma en te Ronse', ibid., 32 (1983), 221–49.

Fig. 3. The Kyrie from the *Missa de Venerabili Sacramento* by Hottinet Barra in the so-called Occo Codex. The manuscript was commissioned about 1530 from the Malines workshop of Petrus van den Hove who had the sobriquet Alamire (A la mi re, i.e. the pitches *a* and *a*^{1} in the hexachord system) by the Amsterdam banker Pompejus Occo, whose arms appear on the right folio. The codex was one of the treasures of the 'Heilige Stede', later called the

Nieuwezijdskapel, where each year the Stille Omgang, or Silent Procession, took place in memory of the miracle of Amsterdam; Pompejus Occo was a *kerkmeester* of the chapel. At the beginning of the superius the monstrance containing the sacred host is depicted in miniature (see also Fig. 14). Brussels, Royal Library, Ms. IV. 922.

Pompejus Occo; it was produced in Flanders in about 1530 and contains Masses by Josquin des Prez, Johannes Mouton, and others (see Fig. 3).[7] Amsterdam, Leiden, Gouda, Delft, and 's-Hertogenbosch had so-called *zeven-getijden* (or daily office) colleges, choirs which consisted of priests and choirboys. Unfortunately we do not always know which compositions the colleges performed. Many choirbooks must have been lost during the religious riots of the sixteenth century. In Leiden they were possibly even cut up at the time of the siege of 1574 and used as emergency money. Thirteen large choirbooks have been preserved from St Peter's Church in Leiden and St John's in 's-Hertogenbosch. Many Netherlands composers are represented in these manuscripts. A bill for book repairs in Delft dated 1523 reads 'Item noch een missael in lombarts formaet en beghint Ja. Obrecht Kyrie' (Item another missal in large format which begins with a Kyrie by Ja. Obrecht).[8] Many details of musical life in 's-Hertogenbosch have been found in the archives of the Illustre Lieve Vrouwe Broederschap; for instance, it is known that Pierre de la Rue and Jacobus Clemens non Papa resided there at some time. Matthaeus Pipelare, Jacobus Barbireau, Crispinus van Stappen, and Nicolas Gombert also played a role in the history of the confraternity.

Details are scarcer concerning Kampen (see Fig. 4), Zwolle, Utrecht, The Hague, Rotterdam, Dordrecht, and Bergen op Zoom. Nevertheless, the existence of a polyphonic tradition in these places can be established. It is almost certain that Jacob Obrecht worked not only in Bergen op Zoom, his presumed birthplace, but also in Utrecht. Erasmus informs us that he sang as a choirboy in Utrecht under Obrecht; he himself stated this in a declaration to the humanist and music theorist Glarean, who taught in Basle.[9]

There were more important centres in the Southern Netherlands. In 1443–4 Antwerp counted Johannes Ockeghem among the singers of the Church of Our Lady, and fifty years later Obrecht. In the sixteenth century the city became one of the most important centres of music printing in the Netherlands, thanks to the publishing houses of Tielman Susato and Christophe Plantin. At this time the foundation was also laid for Antwerp's instrument-making industry. In Bruges the Church of St Donatian was the focus of musical life. This church, destroyed in 1799, once had a very famous choir school; in the fifteenth century instruc-

---

[7] This choirbook was rediscovered in 1972.

[8] See *Bouwstenen voor een geschiedenis der toonkunst in de Nederlanden*, iii (Amsterdam, 1980), 86.

[9] Glarean relates this in his *Dodekachordon*, bk. ii, ch. 11, and in bk. iii, ch. 13; on this disputed passage see C. A. Miller, 'Erasmus on Music', *The Musical Quarterly*, 52 (1966), 343 f.

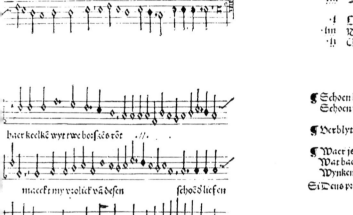

FIG. 4. One of the unbound sheets of the so-called Kamper songbook. It is a unique testimony of activities in the field of music printing in Kampen in the sixteenth century. The sheets were possibly left over from a number printed for an edition of Dutch polyphonic songs, of which no copy survives, but which must have been printed as early as about 1540 (see also Fig. 28). Kampen, Gemeente Archief.

tion there included 'cantus gregorianus, *simpelzank*, and other music, discantus, mensura, musica perfracta, contrapunctum, moteta' among other things.[10] Shortly after 1400, Thomas Fabri, a pupil of the above-mentioned Parisian composer Tapissier, was active as master of the choirboys. The name of Gilles Joye appears for the first time in the chapter minutes of 1451, and he became a ducal chaplain in 1462; a portrait of him, painted by Hans Memling, still survives.[11] Towards the

---

[10] *Die Musik in Geschichte und Gegenwart*, ii (1952), col. 383. The term *simpelzank* must be understood to mean monophonic music; *discantus* is the upper voice in polyphony; *mensura* is the theory of mensural music (see Glossary, 'Mensuration'); *musica perfracta* is the breaking of note-values; *contrapunctum* is counterpoint (see Glossary); and *moteta* is motet (see Glossary).

[11] This is now in the Art Institute, Williamstown, Mass.

end of the fifteenth century Obrecht held the position of singing-master and in the 1540s Clemens non Papa received a probationary appointment. There is little information about musical life in Ghent. The archives of the church authorities, the main employers of composers, have not been systematically studied for this period. However, the town accounts certainly prove that one Willem Obrecht, supposedly the father of Jacob, was municipal trumpeter.

During the time of Margaret of Austria, Malines became the focus of court music. La Rue wrote many French chansons here as court composer. One of the treasures in the town archive is the magnificent codex from the atelier of Petrus Alamire, containing six of La Rue's Masses. As early as 1447 Philip the Good bought a choirbook 'full of new things to sing, such as Masses, motets, and many other items'.[12] Brussels derived its importance in the fifteenth and sixteenth centuries simply from the regular visits of the Burgundian dukes Philip the Fair and Charles V. They were normally attended by the so-called *Chapelle de Bourgogne* or *Chapelle du Roi*. Thomas Crequillon and Nicolas Gombert had connections with the latter. Under the regent, Maria of Hungary, Benedictus Appenzeller had a permanent position as *maître de chapelle* of the court chapel in Brussels. There are few details of the musical history of Tournai and Courtrai during our period. Pierre de Manchicourt and George de la Hèle held the post of *maître de chapelle* in Tournai, while Andreas Pevernage was active in a similar position in Courtrai.

More conspicuous were the towns of Louvain, Liège, and Maastricht, which lie further to the east. As the only university town in the Netherlands, Louvain had a stimulating effect on scholarship in the area. Music formed part of the university curriculum. However, it is uncertain whether the greatest music theorist of the Low Countries, Johannes Tinctoris, studied here.[13] Possibly inspired by the success of Susato, the university bookseller Pierre Phalèse began to print music in 1551. After the death of Susato he associated himself with the Antwerp printer Jean Bellère.

Like Bruges, the cathedral town of Liège had a choir school which contributed greatly to the growth of polyphonic music. In the early fourteenth century Jacobus de Liège wrote his encyclopaedic *Speculum musicae* there; this work closes with an exposition of mensural music. As

Die Musik in Geschichte und Gegenwart, viii (1960), col. 1881.

[13]   e R. Woodley, 'Iohannes Tinctoris: A Review of the Documentary Biographical Evidence', *f the American Musicological Society*, 34 (1981), 217 f.

noted above, Liège was also the birthplace of the first great Netherlands composer, Johannes Ciconia. Amóng the many singers who were active there, Johannes Brassart and Johannes de Limburgia made their names as composers; Arnold and Hugo de Lantins possibly came from this same diocese. Until late in the sixteenth century Liège had close cultural and economic links with Maastricht. This town had already experienced a rich musical life in the Middle Ages thanks to St Gervase's Church and the Church of Our Lady, and in the fifteenth and sixteenth centuries many singers received an education there which prepared them for a career abroad.

In Cambrai, too, musical life was concentrated around the cathedral. This church, dedicated to the Virgin, was one of the greatest architectural achievements in the Netherlands. Dufay occupied a place of honour among the musicians who worked there during the fifteenth century, and in the sixteenth century Johannes Lupi and Jacobus de Kerle were of importance.

The last centre of music in the Low Countries to be mentioned is Lille; until 1477 it was a favourite residence of the Burgundian dukes, and also the town where their central accounts office was established.

2

Sacred Music

THE creative activity of composers from the Low Countries was strongly concentrated on sacred music. When one looks at the works of the most important composers, it is notable that in the fifteenth century the emphasis lay on setting the Ordinary of the Mass, and in the sixteenth century on the motet.

In this chapter attention will be given first to the repertoire in general; the various forms such as the Ordinary and Proper of the Mass, the motet, hymn, psalm and Magnificat, Lamentations, and Passion will be discussed. Subsequently a number of compositional techniques will be examined. The background from which the composer set to work is the subject of the next chapter.

THE REPERTOIRE

Polyphonic music originated in Western Europe in close connection with the celebration of the Mass. In certain centres, particularly the future cathedral towns of France and England, parts of the Mass Propers were performed in polyphony on the great feasts of the Church year. The singer improvised a new part above the chant melody, which functioned as the cantus firmus. The earliest compositions—organa—which have been preserved date from the twelfth century, and are ascribed to Léonin and Pérotin, both of whom were active in Paris. The creation of two- and three-part organa in about 1200 may certainly be seen as one of the most important moments in the history of Western polyphony.

The Mass

It is no surprise that Mass composition was still of central importance two centuries later. Indeed, the celebration of Mass in the Christian Church was regarded as the main element of worship. But in the mean time a change had occurred in the choice of the parts of the Mass set to polyphony. In place of specific texts which were used on the relevant feast-day, and therefore could be sung only once a year, the composer now selected the fixed sections of the Mass: Kyrie, Gloria, Credo, Sanctus, and

Agnus Dei. The precursors of these so-called cyclic Masses date from the fourteenth century; examples are the Mass of Tournai and that by Guillaume de Machaut. There is, however, no hint yet of formal unity; this originated in the fifteenth century, when musical connections were established between the various sections.

Although emphasis is rightly placed on the Ordinary in surveys of Renaissance Mass composition, it is appropriate to begin a description of this repertoire with the Proper, since this part was the first to be set in polyphony. A very important contribution to this genre can be found in seven manuscripts which originated in Trent in northern Italy. This collection includes roughly 1,600 works by about seventy-five composers from the period 1400–75. Almost one sixth of these compositions are based on texts from the Proper, and in a number of cases there is even evidence of cyclic compilation: Introit, Gradual, Alleluia, Offertory, and Communion. The greatest Netherlands contribution to this repertoire came from Dufay. Among the works of this composer there is even a hybrid form, combining Ordinary and Proper, the *Plenarium missae Sancti Jacobi*; the structure of this Mass may be regarded as exceptional in the fifteenth century (just like a similar work by Reginaldus Libert, a probable fellow townsman of Dufay). It consists of an Introit (*Mihi autem nimis*), Kyrie, Gloria, Alleluia (*Hispanorum clarens stella*), Credo, Offertory (*In omnem terram*), Sanctus, Agnus Dei, and Communion (*Vos qui secuti estis me*).

The polyphonic setting of the Mass Propers was imitated by other composers, particularly in German-speaking countries. Heinrich Isaac created a musical and liturgical monument of great scope in his *Choralis constantinus*, named after the chapter of the cathedral in Constance. It comprises almost a hundred Proper cycles based on the texts of major Church feasts, Sundays, and saints' days. These countries remained strongly attached to the use of chant, above all on account of their conservative attitudes; in the light of this, it is hardly surprising that the Proper compositions are based upon the appropriate chant melodies.

The repertoire for the Ordinary of the Mass is remarkably large. More than 500 complete cycles and many individual sections have survived by the fifty composers who are included in the Appendix. Given the relatively limited chance that music had to survive before the introduction of music printing in 1501, it is reasonable to assume that the number of Masses written by these composers was in fact a good deal higher.

In Mass Propers (and naturally also in the motet—see below) the initial words of the text often functioned as an identifying title, but this was not

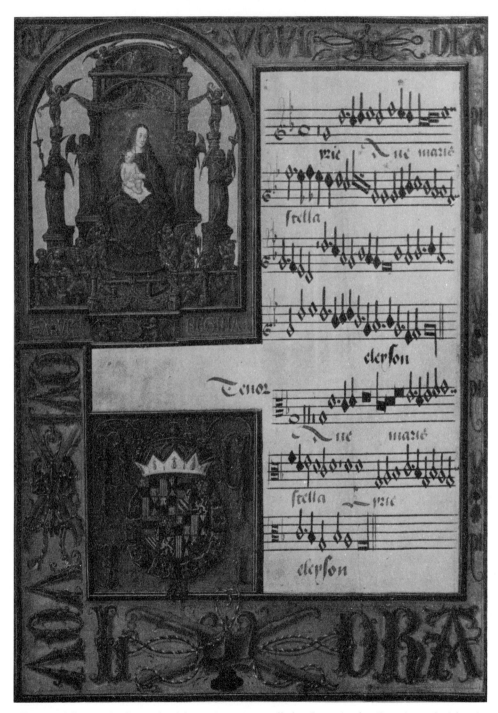

FIG. 5. The Kyrie from the *Missa Ave maris stella* by Josquin des Prez in a choirbook commissioned by Philip the Fair, possibly from Martin Bourgeois. The miniatures were perhaps painted by the Master of the *Hortulus animae*. That on the right-hand page shows

Philip the Fair and Joan of Aragon with their patron saints; on the left-hand page are
Mary, to whom the Mass is dedicated, and the arms of the king. Brussels, Royal Library,
Ms. 9126.

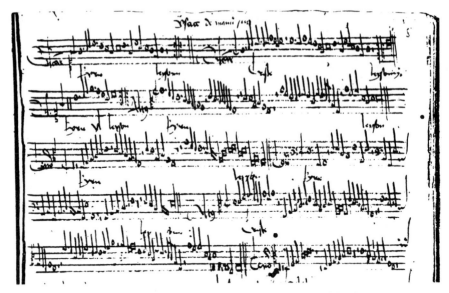

F I G. 6. 'Ysaac de manu sua': this heading above the Kyrie of the *Missa Une musque de Biscaye* by Heinrich Isaac suggests that the composer himself wrote down the music. Berlin, Staatsbibliothek Preussischer Kulturbesitz, Ms. mus. 40021.

the case with the Ordinary of the Mass. As already stated, a unity was achieved between the various sections of the Mass during the fifteenth century; it is worth mentioning here how this happened. Following common practice in earlier polyphony, the composer based his polyphonic setting of the five sections of the Mass on pre-existent musical material, either a simple melody or a polyphonic composition. The title of the Mass was generally taken from the opening words of the model. A frequently heard title is, for example, *Missa L'homme armé*, so called after the popular monophonic song 'L'homme armé doibt on doubter' (see pp. 27 and 58); this is shown in Ex. 1. Examples of Masses named after polyphonic models are encountered mainly in the sixteenth century. Adrian Willaert's *Missa Gaude Barbara*, for instance, was called after the motet of the same name by his Parisian teacher Jean Mouton.

The scoring of these Masses was mainly vocal and generally for four to six voices or parts. But settings for three, seven, and eight to twelve voices, though less common, are not exceptional. The number of voices may vary within the various sections of the composition. Particularly in the Agnus Dei the number of voices was frequently increased to achieve a climax. In Obrecht there is even an example of a remarkable technique in which the scoring is increased progressively: in his *Missa Sub tuum*

EX. I

presidium the Kyrie is for three voices, and in each subsequent section a voice is added so that the Mass ends with seven voices (see p. 66).

The text of the Mass is almost invariably that of the Roman liturgy. Nevertheless, there are variants: occasionally so-called tropes were inserted, by the composer or someone else, or certain articles of the Credo were omitted. Tropes were textual additions to already existing melismatic liturgical melodies; they are found as early as the tenth century. They became popular to the point of threatening to put the liturgical text itself completely in the background, and were therefore banned for ever from the missal and breviary in 1563 during the Council of Trent. In a few Renaissance manuscripts one can see places where, for example, in the Gloria the italicized words in the phrase 'Quoniam tu solus Sanctus *Mariam sanctificans, Mariam gubernans, Mariam coronans* Jesu Christe' have been erased and replaced by the original text, 'tu solus Dominus, tu solus Altissimus'. The *Missa Verbum incarnatum* by Arnold de Lantins has survived with a troped Kyrie and Sanctus. The beginning of the text of its Kyrie gives an example of the character and length of such a trope:

> Kyrie. Verbum incarnatum
> A prophetis nuntiatum
> Pro salute hominum. Kyrie eleison.
> Kyrie. Panis angelorum,
> Lux et decus viatorum,
> Processisti ex Vergine. Kyrie eleison.
> Kyrie. In tua nativitate
> Angelis cum claritate
> Decantabant dulciter. Kyrie eleison.

> Lord. Word incarnate
> Foretold by the prophets
> For the salvation of men. Lord have mercy.
> Lord. Bread of angels,
> Light and ornament to travellers,

You came forth of a Virgin. Lord have mercy.
Lord. At your birth
The angels sang
With a clear and sweet voice. Lord have mercy.

In the second half of the fifteenth century the Netherlanders working in Milan sometimes inserted free motet texts in the Sanctus or in place of it, following the use of the so-called Ambrosian liturgy. This Eucharistic music was probably heard during the consecration. Its musical structure was often kept simple, as in the case of Josquin's *Tu solus qui facis mirabilia* in his *Missa D'ung aultre amer*, and this certainly contributed to the emphasis on this elevated moment in the liturgy. Loyset Compère and Gaspar van Weerbecke each wrote three so-called *Motetti missales* for the same rite. These cycles for the great feasts of the Church year comprise eight motets, which were performed instead of the chants of the Ordinary and Proper of the Mass. One of the cycles by Weerbecke carries the heading 'in honorem sancti spiritus'.

When articles from the text of the Credo were left out, this may have been because of political, social, and religious developments.[1] Several councils discussed the dogmas set out in the Credo. During that held in Basle (1431–49) the nations met to discuss the temporal power of the papacy and the conciliar theory, according to which a general council under divine appointment is the highest ecclesiastical authority, and the Pope only the foremost servant of the Church. The 'Caput' Masses of Dufay (?), Ockeghem, and Obrecht could well have originated in the context of this problem, and also perhaps in that of the choice of Pope. Often in these Masses and in 'L'homme armé' Masses, the articles concerning the Holy Spirit (Articles 13–15) are omitted; the explanation may be found in the quest for unity with the Eastern Church, which was opposed to Roman Catholic teaching regarding the relationship of the Holy Spirit to the other Persons of the Trinity (see p. 59).

The Mass for the departed eventually assumed a special place in the repertoire. This Mass has the following sections: Introit (*Requiem aeternam*), Kyrie, Gradual (*Requiem aeternam*), Tract (*Absolve Domine*), Sequence (*Dies irae, dies illa*), Offertory (*Domine Jesu Christe*), Sanctus, Agnus Dei, Communion (*Lux aeterna*). Before the Council of Trent alternative texts were also used for the Gradual and Tract. Of about forty polyphonic

---

[1] On this theory see R. Hannas, 'Concerning Deletions in the Polyphonic Mass Credo', *Journal of the American Musicological Society*, 5 (1952), 155–86.

Requiem Masses which have been preserved from before 1600, those written by Netherlanders are the most important in terms of both number and quality. Dufay's will states that 'on the day after his burial twelve or more able men' should sing his Requiem; this composition has been lost. The earliest surviving Requiem is by Ockeghem. It is moreover noteworthy that Antoine Brumel's Requiem contains the first polyphonic *Dies irae*, and that the setting by La Rue has an unusually low bass part which falls to *B'♭*.

The Motet

Apart from the texts of the Mass Ordinary and Propers, the composers of the Low Countries were intensely occupied with other texts from the liturgy and also with texts from the Bible and from contemporary prayerbooks. The music historian generally uses the collective noun 'motet' for compositions of this second category. This term is derived from *motetus*, the name of the part above the tenor in thirteenth-century music: the French word *mot* formed the basis of this designation, since French tropes were applied beneath the melismatic upper voices of an existing Latin polyphonic composition. Yet it is possible to subdivide the gigantic motet repertoire in a more detailed manner. A considerable proportion of the texts is taken from the liturgy, and these can be further categorized on the basis of their character and function.

In the fifteenth century antiphons, sequences, hymns, and the Magnificat were frequently set to polyphony. All these categories have a place in the liturgy. The sequence is a type of trope which was added to the Alleluia in the Mass, and later developed into an independent form; a hymn is likewise an original poetic text, which in the Middle Ages grew into a strophic song. Johannes de Limburgia was perhaps the first Netherlander to make an important contribution to the extensive Magnificat repertoire, with five settings. In three works he used alternatim technique, in which the odd-numbered chant verses alternate with the even-numbered polyphonic verses (see p. 31). The 'Salve regina' is the most frequently encountered of all the antiphons. This song originated in the eleventh century, and its great popularity in the Renaissance influenced the development of confraternities dedicated to the veneration of the Virgin. One of the most notable such confraternities was the Guild of Our Lady in Antwerp. Obrecht and Noel Bauldeweyn were both members, and they wrote several 'Salve regina' settings. That by Bauldeweyn cites the rondeau *Je n'ay dueil* by Ockeghem in the superius; in its new context this love lament refers to the Mother of Sorrows. Between 1425 and 1550

FIG. 7. Fragment from Orlando di Lasso's Fourth Penitential Psalm, *Miserere mei, Deus* (Psalm 50) in the magnificent codex (Part 1) belonging to Albrecht V of Bavaria. The miniaturist Hans Mielich expresses the meaning of verse 15, 'Lord, open my lips, and my mouth will speak out your praise' in his depiction of double-choir vocal and instrumental music (see also Fig. 1). Munich, Bayerische Staatsbibliothek, Mus. Ms. A.

Den eerften pfalm. Beatus vir qui non abyt. Nae die wyfe.
Het was een clercxken dat ginck ter fcholen

Alich is die man, en goet gheheten Die tot dē boofen niet en gaet Noch

bi den fpotters is ghefeten Die in haer weghen niet en ftaet.

FIG. 8. The superius of the first *souterlied* by Jacobus Clemens non Papa. It is Psalm 1, *Beatus vir qui non abiit*, in the metrical version by Willem van Zuylen van Nijevelt. The tenor sings the psalm text to the melody 'Het was een clerxken'; the two other voices, superius and bass, are newly composed. Clemens's *Souter-liedekens* were published by Tielman Susato in Antwerp in 1556. The Hague, Koninklijke Bibliotheek.

the Netherlanders composed more than 125 polyphonic settings of the 'Salve regina'.

Towards the end of the fifteenth century the polyphonic setting of psalm texts began to develop, particularly on account of Josquin's contribution to this genre. Works which use an entire psalm text, including doxology, display a liturgical function. But there are also many psalm motets based on compilations of verses from one or more psalms, and these compositions must be regarded as paraliturgical. A few complete polyphonic psalters were composed during the sixteenth century, notably by the Netherlanders Jacobus Clemens non Papa (the Dutch *Souterliedekens*; see Fig. 8) and Jan Pieterszoon Sweelinck.

Lamentations and Passions are also liturgical in function. The earliest polyphonic settings of these Holy Week texts date from the second half of the fifteenth century. Netherlanders contributed to both genres: sensitive settings of the Lamentations of Jeremiah by Johannes Tinctoris, Pierre de la Rue, and Orlando di Lasso are known. Lasso also set the Passion narratives of all four evangelists. Whether the *St Matthew Passion* found in almost twenty sixteenth-century sources can be correctly ascribed to Obrecht is a musicologically contentious issue.

Texts of polyphonic sacred music which were not taken from the liturgy or Scripture were mostly borrowed from devotional books or original poetry. Beside numerous motets based on prayers of a private nature, devotional texts of a more liturgical tone were also set. An important example is the *Preces speciales* of Jacobus de Kerle, composed for the Council of Trent. Kerle took ten Latin poems by Petrus de Soto, a professor in theology at Dillingen, as the texts of these motets. During the Council certain abuses in church music were discussed; partly because of the *Preces* of Kerle, the Council decided not to prohibit polyphony in church. While the *Preces* are both textually and musically connected with church music proper, many examples of the fifteenth-century ceremonial motet have a style all of their own. As Church and State were still so closely related in the late Middle Ages, it is not surprising that both authorities were represented at many solemn occasions. Consequently, the music performed at such festivals was often based on original Latin texts which contained some secular elements. The ceremonial character of this music could be shown to full advantage since loud instruments often performed with the vocal ensemble (see p. 103).

The extent of the motet repertoire that originated with the Netherlands School cannot easily be determined. There were certainly composers who had only a few motets to their name, but in the sixteenth century particularly the number of motets ascribed to a composer often ran into hundreds. Simply counting the pieces says little about the scope of the repertoire itself. The length of motets can vary considerably. For example, the *Ave Maria* by Crispinus van Stappen has fewer than fifty bars, while in contrast Josquin's *Miserere* has 424. So-called motet cycles occupy a particular place in the repertoire; Gaspar van Weerbecke assembled such cycles for Pentecost and some Marian feasts (see p. 22).

In the motet, as in the Mass, the scoring was generally vocal. But as noted above, wind instruments were used for the performance of ceremonial music, and likewise prayer motets, conceived for intimate surroundings, were undoubtedly often performed by a small ensemble of mixed voices and instruments. Arnold de Lantins's *O pulcherrima mulierum* has a texture reasonably typical of the first half of the fifteenth century (see Ex. 2). In the second half of the sixteenth century it was the norm at some wealthy courts, such as Munich and Prague, to score church music for

EX. 2

O pulcherri- ma mu-li-e- rum,

both voices and instruments. It is not impossible that this performance practice developed following the model of the mixed scorings in Venetian double-choir music: the two choir galleries in St Mark's, where Willaert was *maestro di cappella* for so long, sometimes inspired Venetian masters to produce the most spectacular sonorous effects.

COMPOSITIONAL TECHNIQUES

It has been explained above that polyphony originated in the Middle Ages when new parts were improvised or composed above sustained chant notes. The current term for this fundamental part, 'cantus firmus', was seldom used before 1500. It is not even included in Tinctoris's dictionary of about 1475, the *Terminorum musicae diffinitorium*. The original meaning of the term is 'firm voice'. Given the different shapes which a cantus firmus can assume in a polyphonic Renaissance composition, it would be more correct to call the pre-existing melody of a new composition the *cantus prius factus*, or 'already composed melody'; this term seems to have been used for the first time by Franco of Cologne about 1260.

Cantus prius factus

In the music of the Netherlands School the *cantus prius factus* was generally borrowed from chant, but secular song melodies also appear frequently. In the fifteenth century the development of the *cantus prius factus* technique led to a fascinating diversity of musical forms. It is no exaggeration to state that the use of this technique almost completely determined composers' thought in the field of sacred music for a long time. Although the main function of the pre-existent melody in the Mass cycle was as an element which brought about cohesion between the different sections, the composer soon discovered ways of developing rich and elaborate melodic lines in the newly composed parts. While the compositional process was fundamentally horizontal, the sustained notes of the *cantus prius factus* resulted in a cantus firmus in the original sense of the term, and as such guaranteed a vertical relationship between the different parts. A passage from the Kyrie of Dufay's *Missa L'homme armé* illustrates this technique (see Ex. 3).

A third compositional element developed almost naturally from the application of the *cantus prius factus*. In order to strengthen the vertical relationship between the parts, the composer introduced material from the *cantus prius factus* in other voices. This originally consisted of a single chance anticipation, as in the extract from Josquin's *Missa L'homme armé*

EX. 3

EX. 4

super voces musicales shown in Ex. 4. About 1500, however, the technique of imitation developed to such an extent that the cantus firmus technique almost totally disappeared. Instead, pre-existent melodic material could be used in all parts of a composition. The parts became musically more similar to each other and imitated each other continually so that a homogeneous texture was produced. This method can already be seen in the second Mass which Josquin based on the popular 'L'homme armé' melody. Ex. 5, taken from the Kyrie of the *Missa L'homme armé sexti toni*, shows the imitation technique clearly. The titles mentioned above need an explanation. Among other things the word *vox* meant 'note' to medieval music theorists, and therefore the six notes of the Guidonian hexachord could be referred to as *sex voces* or indeed *voces musicales*. In the first Mass Josquin introduced the 'L'homme armé' melody on all the degrees of the *hexachordum naturale*: C = ut (Kyrie), D = re (Gloria), E = mi (Credo),

F = fa (Sanctus), G = sol (Agnus i), A = la (Agnus iii). Compare the
entrance of the theme in the Sanctus (Ex. 6) with that in the Kyrie (Ex. 4).
In his *Missa L'homme armé sexti toni* Josquin places the melody in the sixth
tone, the Hypolydian mode: C–D–E–F–G–A–B–C. However, he trans-
poses the melody up a fourth (to start on F), and therefore the key
signature becomes one flat (see Ex. 5).

EX. 5

The dominant role which the *cantus prius factus* played in fifteenth-
century composition, discussed above, is also expressed visually: the pre-
existent melody in long notes functioned as a primary thread in the
polyphonic texture. While the cantus firmus originally lay in the lowest-
sounding part, its place changed at the beginning of the fifteenth century.
When the number of voices began to extend to four, a contratenor, or
bassus was written under the tenor part, giving the composer greater
harmonic freedom. He no longer felt himself restricted in his harmonic
thought by the obligatory notes of the *cantus prius factus* in the tenor. At
the same time, however, we see another development. The *cantus prius
factus* begins to appear in parts other than the tenor, and not only in long
notes. When the position of the *cantus prius factus* changes in the course of
the composition, it is called a *migrans*. In many compositions the *cantus
prius factus* lies in the highest voice, the superius, and if in such cases the
melody appears in long note-values the music often assumes an imposing
monumental character. Obrecht used this procedure in his *Missa Sub tuum
praesidium* (see Ex. 7). The Marian antiphon is heard like a chorale high
above the other voices. Its effect is similar to that of the striking ripieno
soprano entry of 'O Lamm Gottes unschuldig' in the opening chorus of
Bach's *St Matthew Passion*. At the same time the particular placing of the
chant antiphon recalls the image of the Virgin with her cloak: 'Under your
protection [cloak] we flee, O Holy Mother of God.'[2]

---

[2] See J. Timmers, *Symboliek en iconographie der christelijke kunst* (Roermond, 1947), 495.

EX. 6

EX. 7

(Reprinted from *Jacob Obrecht Opera Omnia editio altera*, vi, with the permission of the Vereniging voor Nederlandse Muziekgeschiedenis.)

Paraphrase

The *cantus prius factus* technique was generally employed in two different ways: either the melody was substantially unchanged and used in long note-values, or its notes functioned as the basis for a new melody. In the latter case it was freely adopted by means of interpolations and ornamentation. This type of quotation is called 'paraphrase technique': the original and the new notes join to create a homogeneous melodic style. The Netherlanders frequently used this technique. In the first half of the fifteenth century the paraphrased melody was most often placed in the upper voice. A fine example of this method is found in Dufay's *Alma redemptoris mater*, quoted in Ex. 8. In order to illustrate how the composer changed the shape of his chant model, the notes of the original are indicated with a cross in this extract.

It is likely that, while in Savoy, Dufay wrote a number of hymns for the court chapel; paraphrase technique is an essential element in these works. The compositions are for three voices, and the medieval melody lies in the

EX. 8

EX. 9

upper voice. The close relationship with the liturgical chant is demonstrated in the fact that the verses of the text were performed in alternatim, that is, alternating monodic chant and polyphony. Alternatim performance had already occurred in the earliest centuries of Christendom in the psalmody of the Eastern Church, and it was also used in settings of the Mass Ordinary and the Magnificat.

Paraphrase technique left its mark on the polyphony of the Netherlands School for almost two centuries. It proved to be an ideal means for combining old and new musical material, and the composer's inventiveness moreover guaranteed an almost endless variety of melodic forms based on the revered liturgical chants. Exx. 9 and 10 show two passages from Josquin's works which illustrate the variety of this procedure. In his four-part double antiphon *Alma redemptoris mater | Ave regina celorum* the two chant melodies combine to form counterpoint (Ex. 9). It is interesting to compare Josquin's 'version' of *Alma* with that by Dufay (Ex. 8). In Josquin's five-part *Salve regina* the first four notes of the antiphon function as an ostinato motif in the *quinta vox*, while the four other voices often accommodate different fragments of the original melody (Ex. 10).

In the fifteenth century the *cantus prius factus* technique gave rise to unprecedented formal structures. While in motets the pre-existent melody was generally presented only once, in a cyclic Mass the basic melody was heard many times. Two of the many possible methods of presentation are dealt with here. There are six anonymous Masses based on 'L'homme armé' in the Burgundian manuscript VI E 40 of the Biblioteca Nazionale in Naples, and these combine to form a cycle. The song melody is divided into five segments, each of which forms the *cantus prius factus* for one Mass;

the sixth Mass, which concludes the cycle, uses the complete melody. This is a unique compositional achievement. It is tempting to suggest that the Masses were performed on six consecutive days, so that the complete 'L'homme armé' melody contributed to making the final Mass the climax of the cycle. The second example is found in the works of Obrecht. One of his Masses is based on a German song to Mary, 'Maria zart'. The composer has broken the melody in thirteen segments and placed them in their original order throughout the first four sections of the Mass. A climactic point is achieved in this structure too: in the Agnus Dei the entire melody is heard as many as three times, first in the bass, then as a *migrans*, and finally in the superius.

EX. 10

Isoperiodicity

One of the most remarkable applications of the *cantus prius factus* technique in the fifteenth century is encountered in the so-called isoperiodic (from the Greek *isos*: alike) structures. This term implies that the composer repeats material, both melodic and rhythmic. What is meant by this? The essence of the procedure is clearly explained in an instruction written about 1300 by the Parisian theorist Johannes de Grocheo: 'The tenor [of the composition] is the voice on which all the others are based, just as the parts of a house or building are erected on the foundations. This voice is the gauge, and it fixes the extent of the parts.'[3]

The accuracy of this approach to polyphonic composition in the Middle Ages is demonstrated by the fact that the *ars musicae* was one of the arts in

---

[3] See E. Rohloff, *Der Musiktraktat des Johannes Grocheo*, Media Latinitas Musica, ii (Leipzig, 1943), 57.

FIG. 9. Woodcut by Hans Holbein (1523), inspired by Revelation 11: 1: 'Go and measure God's sanctuary'. With these words John predicts that a new temple will be built in Jerusalem. In the fifteenth century 'measuring' could also play a role in composition. The papal tiara on the head of the dragon expresses anti-papal feelings.

the quadrivium, namely a technical science (see p. 136). The art of music was consequently depicted in this manner: a miniature by Jehan de Nizières in Corbichon's *Livre des propriétés des choses* of about 1400 shows a group of singers and instrumentalists, while in the foreground are painted numbers, a pair of scales, a triangle, and a yard-stick. Once polyphonic music was notated in choirbooks, after 1250, the tenor with its long notes was written at the foot of the page, and the other parts above.

EX. II

The term 'isoperiodic' (or 'isorhythmic') is used in modern musicology to indicate that the tenor—not necessarily taken from an existing melody—is built on melodic and/or rhythmic patterns which are repeated a number of times. In medieval music theory these patterns were called *color* and *talea* respectively. *Color* and *talea* can occur in combination with each other, in which case they generally overlap. In the fifteenth century, however, they also appeared independently. The consequences of the application of this procedure for a composition can be illustrated with the help of Dufay's motet *Supremum est mortalibus bonum*, written in 1433 for the celebration of the peace treaty between Pope Eugenius IV and King Sigismund. This three-part composition is based on a freely composed cantus firmus which consists of two *colores* (*color* I is repeated exactly) and six *taleae* (each *color* is built on three identical rhythmic periods). In schematic form we see the following:

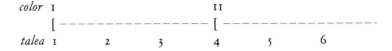

Each *talea* consists of fifteen bars. In Ex. 11 *taleae* I and II are written out one beneath the other. The text of the motet is an isometric poem. The lines are divided into groups of two to four over the *taleae*, according to the importance of their contents. The procedure described so graphically by Johannes de Grocheo is here carried out in practice.

The technique of isoperiodicity developed in the French motet repertoire of the fourteenth century. Not only composers from the Low

Countries, but also those in England assimilated this formal principle, sometimes showing this in extremely refined ways in their compositions. This is especially the case where complete rhythmic complexes are repeated not only in the tenor, but also in the upper voices, while the melodic development of the music changes. Dufay's motet *Vasilissa, ergo gaude* of 1420, conceived according to the principle of the Golden Section (see p. 60), gives an example of this (see Ex. 12).

EX. 12

Concupivit rex decorem tuum   Quoniam ipse est dominus tuus

Other Netherlanders who used isoperiodicity included Ciconia (above all in his ceremonial compositions) and Binchois. In the second half of the fifteenth century this procedure made way for new formal principles, but simple forms of *color* and *talea* remained a structural element until the middle of the sixteenth century. When the composer resorted to this technique it frequently resulted in music of an exceptional standard. In Obrecht's *Missa Sub tuum praesidium*, mentioned above, the Marian antiphon of the same name appears in each of the five sections of the Mass, and in this way assumes the character of a *color*.

Josquin also composed some of his motets according to the ancient principle of *color* and *talea*. For instance, he based his Marian motet *Ave nobilissima creatura* and his Jesus motet *Huc me sydereo* on the same chant melody, which is repeated three times in each composition. The similarity between the two works goes even further than this. Although the chant *cantus prius factus* has a different text in each of the motets, the antiphon melodies still prove to be identical. The note-values of the *cantus prius factus* are proportionally shortened with each repetition. It was even possible to notate the tenor melody only once, using three different mensuration signs. In *Ave nobilissima* this part reads as in Ex. 13.

The same procedure is found in Gombert's lament on the death of Josquin. This motet, *Musae Iovis*, is based on a chant invitatory from the office of the dead, 'Circumdederunt me gemitus mortis . . .' (The sighs of death surrounded me . . .). In the fourfold presentation of this *cantus prius factus* the note-values are related to each other in the ratio of $4 : 2 : 1 : 3$, and the number of 'bars' for which this part rests before each entry of the cantus firmus is also proportionally defined on each occasion. Gombert's lament was almost certainly written in the 1520s. In 1539 Willaert's first collection of five-part motets was published; it contains the hymn of praise *Ave Maria, ancilla Sanctae Trinitatis*. Here again there is still evidence of an isoperiodic procedure: the chant antiphon 'Ave Maria gratia plena' is heard eleven times in succession with few rests in between. Since the note-values in the tenth and eleventh statements are halved while in the others they remain unchanged, the two *partes* of the motet are of the same length. In the *prima pars* the *color* with its *talea* are heard five times, and in the *secunda pars* six.

EX. 13

Be-ne-di-cta   tu   in   mu-li-e-ri-bus

Soggetto ostinato

When the composer chooses only a short motif as the basis for his work and then uses it frequently in a single voice, the part in question assumes what could be called an 'obstinate' character. The device which in this case determines the form of the work is called *soggetto ostinato*. This technique was used as early as the thirteenth century, and became common since it lent itself well to the imitation of bird-calls. A telling example of the imitation of the cuckoo appears in the Mass by Johannes Martini named after this bird, where the tenor sings 'cuckoo' almost incessantly (see Ex. 14).

A similar *imitazione della natura* appears in the *Missa Stephane gloriose* by Pierre Moulu. In the six-part Agnus Dei III the ostinato motif sol–fa–mi–fa–sol–re is heard in two voices. While in the first tenor it is sung at the same pitch over and again, it descends stepwise at each statement in the second. The meaning is clear: St Stephen, the first martyr, died by stoning, and the falling nature of the six-note motif represents the stones.

The works of Dufay include two settings of the Gloria based on an ostinato tenor. Throughout the four-part *Gloria ad modum tubae* (in the manner of a *tuba*, i.e. a trumpet) two natural trumpets alternate with a fanfare motif consisting of the harmonics above low *C* (see Ex. 15). The method which Dufay put into practice in this Gloria derives from the form of the fourteenth-century Italian caccia, whose text deals with hunting: the two upper voices sing the text in canon above an instrumental tenor part.

EX. 14

EX. 15

Josquin used the ostinato technique in a more impressive way than any other composer. His psalm *Miserere* was admired everywhere in the sixteenth century, partly on account of the intense effect that stems from a motif set to the text of the prayer 'Miserere mei, Deus' (Have mercy on me, O God, in your goodness). This motif, sung *recto tono*, falls stepwise through an octave; it then rises and falls again. In this way the ostinato functions as a reminder of the background against which the psalm text must be understood. In his five-part Marian antiphon *Salve regina* (see p. 31), the chant incipit is heard twenty-four times, and numerically forms the basis of a piece of music in which a deep sense of symbolism may be perceived (see p. 82).

There are two six-part settings from the middle of the sixteenth century by Clemens non Papa and Orlando di Lasso which recount the biblical story of the raising of Lazarus (John 11): *Fremuit spiritu Jesus . . .* Here, too, the ostinato cry, 'Lazare, veni foras' (Lazarus, come forth), has a meaningful connection with the subject of the motet.

Soggetto cavato

For Josquin it was only a small step from *soggetto ostinato* to *soggetto cavato*; he seems to have been the first to use this new structural principle. The term, introduced by Gioseffo Zarlino in 1558, indicates that the theme is 'excavated', in this case from words in which the vowels are treated as the solmization syllables of the Guidonian hexachord in order to form a melody. One may perhaps regard Josquin's *Missa La sol fa re mi* (*Missa Laise faire moy?*) as a bridge between *soggetto ostinato* and *soggetto cavato* technique. The theme indicated in the title occurs no less than 237 times in the Mass, but there is none the less no trace of monotony! The classic example of the new procedure, however, is Josquin's *Missa Hercules dux Ferrarie*. This Mass, dedicated to Ercole I d' Este, is built on the theme re–ut–re–ut–re–fa–mi–re, which is derived from the vowels in the duke's title. Despite the simplicity of the theme, which is heard in changing note-values and at different pitches, the music has a majestic character. No wonder this 'invention' also inspired later composers. Remarkably enough the Mass survived with other titles in two magnificent codices. To judge from the words 'Philippus rex Castillie', which appear under the *soggetto* of the Kyrie in Ms. 9126 of the Royal Library in Brussels, Philip the Fair wished to associate this Mass with himself; this was also the case with Frederick the Wise, Duke of Saxony—in Ms. 3 of the University Library in Jena the same *soggetto* is connected with the words 'Fridericus dux Saxsonie'. It is clear, however, that it is no longer a question of *soggetto cavato* in these last two works.

Canon

Though polyphony by Netherlands composers does not reveal its musical nature in 'learned' compositional techniques on first hearing, the use of canonic counterpoint has time and again caught the imagination of those fascinated by this music. As early as 1547 the Swiss theorist Glarean published an anthology of such canons in his *Dodecachordon*, and he praised those who devised them for their skill. The great Czech music historian of the nineteenth century A. W. Ambros spoke rightly of 'die Künste der Niederländer'.

Under the entry 'fuga' in Tinctoris's dictionary (mentioned above) one finds a description of what we would nowadays term 'canon': '. . . a perfect agreement between the parts of a composition as to the value, the name, the shape, and sometimes even the placing of their notes and rests'. He defines the Greek and Latin word 'canon' as '. . . a directive which makes the intention of the composer clear in a somewhat obscure manner'. It can scarcely be coincidental that the present-day term 'canon' began to replace the older term in about 1550: the complexity and subtlety of the Netherlands canonic art have never been exceeded in the history of Western music. This fact, combined with the practice of giving the key to the solution of these *fugae* in a 'canon', led directly to the change of name.

Two exceptionally difficult puzzle canons by Johannes Ciconia belong to the earliest examples of Netherlands canonic technique. However, the first composer to use the technique more frequently was Dufay. In his four-part Marian motet *Inclita stella maris* the two upper voices are notated as a single part in *tempus imperfectum*, while a Latin motto indicates that the melody must be performed in *tempus perfectum* at the same time. Because the breve is divided into two and three semibreves respectively in these two mensuration signs, while the other notes share a common value, there is a gradual shift in the relationship between the parts.

EX. 16

Working from the same principle, Ockeghem produced a masterly proof of his skill in the *Missa Prolationum*. This four-part composition is notated in two parts. The note-values of one pair are defined by *tempus imperfectum* and *perfectum cum prolatione minore*, and those of the other by *tempus imperfectum* and *perfectum cum prolatione maiore*. What is the result of this? The gap between the pair formed by the second and fourth voices and their two higher companions slowly widens just as in the Dufay motet. But Ockeghem goes a step further. He also widens the interval between the entries of the higher of the vocal pairs by a tone in each successive section of the Mass Ordinary: the first canons of Kyrie I are in unison, those of the Osanna at the octave. Ex. 16 shows the mensuration canons at the fifth at the beginning of the Credo.

For the sixteenth century, a perfect example of a three-part mensuration canon was the Agnus Dei II from Josquin's *Missa L'homme armé super voces musicales*. This short canon, with its perfectly balanced melody, was included in several works of music theory with a Latin motto that linked it with the symbolism of the Trinity (see p. 71). A contemporary of Josquin added a fourth mensuration sign to the canon, and the piece was depicted

FIG. 10. Inlay work in wood showing a proportion canon from Josquin's *Missa L'homme armé super voces musicales*. The anonymous artist has taken a Latin couplet instead of the Agnus Dei; it can be translated as follows, 'This [i.e. Josquin's] well-known talent has brought all the arts to life and the whole world rejoices in eternal song.' Choir-stall, Basilica of S Sisto, Piacenza.

in this form on the back of a choir-stall in the Basilica of S Sisto in Piacenza in 1514 (see Fig. 10).[4]

Ockeghem's *Missa Prolationum* can also be correctly called a *missa ad fugam*, a Mass which is composed entirely on canonic principles. Antoine Brumel designed his *Missa A l'ombre d'ung buissonnet* along these lines, though not with mensuration canons: the double-canon technique is used in all the four-part sections, and the counterpoint arises wholly from the amalgamation of two two-part canons. Two *missae ad fugam* by Josquin are known in which both of the two parts are treated canonically throughout. Canonic technique is also used in the most varied manner in Isaac's four- and six-part Masses on the song 'Comment peult avoir joye'. This compositional principle also plays a significant role in the works of La

    [4] My colleague Jaap van Benthem discovered this in 1972; see his article 'Einige Musikintarsien des frühen 16. Jahrhunderts in Piacenza und Josquins Proportionskanon "Agnus Dei"', *Tijdschrift van de Vereniging voor Nederlandse Muziekgeschiedenis*, 24 (1974), 97–111.

FIG. 11. The autograph of the four-voice canon *Miserere mei, Domine* by Jan Pieterszoon Sweelinck. After his death a short text was written under the second stave, praising the composer for his exceptional skills. Lübeck, Bibliothek der Hansestadt, Ms. 61b.

Rue. The *Missa O salutaris hostia* is one of his masterpieces: it proves to be completely canonic in all five sections, and the composer even derives four voices from a single notated part. However, his *Missa Ave sanctissima Maria* is the most magnificent: this Mass, enriched with copious tropes in various manuscripts, is considered to be the earliest *missa ad fugam* in which six voices are derived from three parts. The work parodies (see

p. 46) his motet of the same name, which opens one of the splendidly illuminated collections of chansons belonging to his patroness, Margaret of Austria. The beginning of the Kyrie offers an example of one of the triple canons (see Ex. 17).

The delight in inventing canonic counterpoint led two of the above-named Netherlands composers to exceptional feats. In his psalm motet

EX. 17

Qui habitat in adjutorio Altissimi Josquin managed to write a quadruple canon in which each part gives rise to six voices. The parts enter from top to bottom, with superius, alto, tenor, and bass singing the first eight verses of Psalm 91. Only after sixty-four bars does the twenty-fourth voice make its entrance. At the line 'Though a thousand fall at your side, ten thousand at your right hand . . .' an almost full texture is reached.[5] One of Ockeghem's compositions is also a quadruple canon, constructed according to the same scheme. In his piece up to nine voices may be derived from one part, but the end-result is more limited than in Josquin: when the first tenor enters, the ninth soprano begins a lengthy final note. Also, the composition lacks a text; but its meaning is shown by the title, *Deo gratias!* (See p. 72).

Faux-bourdon

We now take a step backwards in the history of the Netherlands School to describe the so-called faux-bourdon technique. Scarcely any other musical phenomenon from this period has caused so many musicological con-

---

[5] Josquin's *Qui habitat* was performed at my request by several choirs under the direction of Felix de Nobel in St Mark's, Venice, in 1972.

troversies. Discussions concerning the explanation of the term and the procedure stand in sharp contrast to the simplicity of the device itself.

The compositions in which this technique is employed date from the period 1425 to 1500, and they are very limited in number. Most of the composers of these works came from the Low Countries and France; Dufay, with his twenty-four compositions, was more prolific than any of the others.

What does 'faux-bourdon' mean? The term is first encountered about 1425 in two-part compositions, as a 'canon' or instruction for the singers who must add a third part. When Dufay introduced this procedure in the Communion of his *Missa Sancti Jacobi*, he explained it as follows: 'When you wish to have a three-part piece, then take the notes of the upper voice and begin at the same time a fourth lower.' The small notes in Ex. 18 show the realization of the third part (the crosses above the notes in the superius indicate the chant melody).

EX. 18

In practice faux-bourdon inevitably led to a very simple type of counterpoint. The doubling of the upper voice in parallel fourths, a method which recalls the origins of polyphony in the twelfth century, limits the tenor's freedom of movement: apart from brief dissonances only the intervals of the sixth and octave from the superius are permitted. Harmonically speaking, 6-3 chords predominate, and these lend the music a sweet and consonant, though fairly monotonous character. It is therefore understandable that the procedure was only used on a small scale. (For a hypothesis concerning the symbolic interpretation of this, see p. 61–2.)

The term 'faux-bourdon' probably originated in entomology: in French, *faux bourdon* means a drone. It will be explained below that the text of Dufay's Communion *Vos qui secuti estis me* has been associated in medieval thought with the bee (see p. 62).

Faux-bourdon was preferred in simple liturgical compositions, such as hymns, psalms and Magnificats, in which the polyphonic verses alternated with chant. However, there are some motets, such as Dufay's *Supremum est mortalibus bonum* (mentioned above) of which short sections are written in this striking harmony; the procedure is also found in the works of Binchois, Busnois, Johannes de Limburgia, and Martini. The influence of this technique on later Western music is clear from the fact that the term 'faux-bourdon' is still generally used for sequences of 6-3 chords.

Through-imitation

It has been shown in the section *'Cantus prius factus'* above that imitation came to take the place of the cantus firmus technique about 1500. Both are linked with the new search for greater homogeneity between the various parts in the texture generated by the polyphonic treatment of melodies. Linear composition, whereby the various parts of a piece were successively devised to fit with a given *cantus prius factus*, began gradually to give way to a more simultaneous creative process. This development went hand in hand with a change in harmonic thought, which involved an increasing concentration on the vertical relationship between the parts. Composers now became preoccupied with the creation of balance between the parts. There seem to have been parallel developments in contemporary Italian architecture, and in this connection L. B. Alberti's definition of beauty should be quoted: 'Beauty consists in a rational integration of the proportions of all the parts of a building in such a way that every part has its absolutely fixed size and shape and nothing could be added or taken away without destroying the harmony of the whole.'[6] This definition had a great effect on fifteenth-century Italian architecture, and when we realize that the principle of through-imitation developed mainly as a result of Josquin's long period of work in Italy, it is tempting to consider a possible connection. Indeed, the procedures in both cases are based on the laws of strict symmetry and classical balance.

The technique of through-imitation is an almost logical consequence of the development mentioned on p. 28 above, namely the use of melodic material from an existing song in all parts of the composition to create imitation between the parts. The search for symmetry meant that the *cantus prius factus* had to resemble the other parts in its rhythmic aspect as well. This was only possible if the *cantus prius factus* was no longer presented in long note-values. Eventually copious insertions were made to avoid the frequent repetition of the *cantus prius factus*. Josquin's *Missa Pange lingua* may be seen as an early high-point in this process of change. The chant of the hymn of that name forms the basic material of the

---

[6] Quoted in R. Wittkower, *Architectural Principles in the Age of Humanism* (4th edn., London, 1974), 7.

composition; it is divided into six short phrases, which in their turn
provide the seeds for the unfolding of new melodies. The first three
phrases of the hymn and their appearance in the four voices of the Kyrie
is schematically represented in Ex. 19. (Unbroken lines represent the
paraphrased hymn chant; dotted lines indicate unrelated material. The
absence of a line signifies rests.)

EX. 19

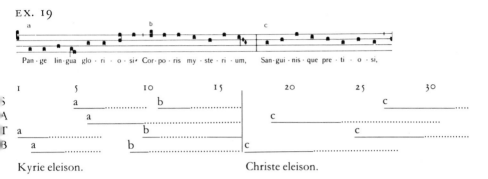

Kyrie eleison.   Christe eleison.

Another important aspect emerges at the entries of themes 'a' and 'c'.
The melody and the intervals at 'a' between tenor and bass parts on the
one hand, and between superius and alto on the other are identical for
some bars; likewise, the bass is paired with the alto, and the tenor with the
superius at the entries of theme 'c'. This is referred to as 'paired imitation'.
This remarkable form of imitation came into vogue in about 1500, and
proved before long to be a favourite method of introducing a certain
transparency to compositions which were constructed primarily on the
principle of through-imitation. Josquin has been cited more than any
other composer as having shown a preference for this procedure.

Although at first composers willingly based their works on existing
melodic material, in the sixteenth century they increasingly distanced
themselves from this technique. It is not impossible that the motet, with
its choice of texts, offered a much greater range of possibilities than Mass
composition, and that this brought about the fundamental change. Many
sixteenth-century motets prove to be based on contemporary prayers and
on biblical passages which had never been provided with melodies of their
own when used in a liturgical context. Psalm motets come to mind as an
example. Moreover, under the influence of humanism, the composer came
to regard the expression of emotions as one of the most important facets
of creative activity. The less he was attached to musical points of
departure, the more fully this objective could be realized.

When the principle of through-imitation was observed thoroughly,

EX. 20

each successive section of text acquired its own melodic identity, and all voices of the composition shared the same musical material. The rhythm and inflexions of the Latin words determined the shape of the musical motifs. Thus not only the general atmosphere of the text, but also specific parts of it were expressed by musical means. By way of illustration, Ex. 20 shows two passages from the motet *Vox in Rama* by Clemens non Papa: 'A voice was heard in Ramah, sobbing and loudly lamenting . . .' (Matthew 2: 18).

By the time of Josquin's death imitative technique had reached a level which was never surpassed. Many composers followed in his footsteps and used this procedure well into the seventeenth century. But other paths were followed as well, for example by Willaert and Lasso. The motets of masters such as Philippus de Monte and Jan Pieterszoon Sweelinck, however, were still largely based on this type of writing.

Parody

Parody is the last to be discussed here of the many compositional techniques practised by the Netherlanders. The technique involves the use of existing polyphonic music in a new composition; as early as the fifteenth century there were hints of this principle, but it became very popular only about 1530.

As far as is known, the term 'parody Mass' was first used in 1587 in a work by the German composer Jacob Paix, which took a motet by Crecquillon as its starting-point. The title of this composition is: *Missa parodia mutetae 'Domine da nobis' Thomas Crequillonis senis vocibus* (parody Mass on Thomas Crecquillon's motet *Domine da nobis* for six voices). For Aristotle the word 'parody' meant an amusing adaptation of a serious literary work, something quite different from the definition understood in sixteenth-century music, and it might therefore seem strange that in music history the old terms such as *Missa ad imitationem* . . . and *Missa super* . . . have fallen into disuse. In his treatise *Rerum musicarum opusculum*, published in 1535, Johannes Froschius deals with parody methods and uses the terms *copia* and *imitatio Authorum*. The writer even suggests that one should transcribe the best passages from the work of others, so that they can be incorporated into one's own compositions in due course.

Because the preference for parody technique was demonstrated mainly in settings of the long texts of the Mass, it seems reasonable to assume that its popularity resulted from a certain antipathy to the continual need to clothe the same texts in new music. Freely chosen motet texts must have offered a far greater stimulus to new musical invention, and the composer's work must have felt easier with an attractive chanson or madrigal or a well-written motet on the desk.

Just as frequent repetitions of the *cantus prius factus* were avoided in through-imitation, so the composer broke his model into a number of sections which were inserted at crucial moments in the Mass composition, and which were separated from each other by short or long interpolations. At the beginning of each section of a Mass the beginning of the model can normally be heard. In the long sections of the Mass particular groups of themes may be used more than once. Obviously in the parody process the model may undergo all types of modifications so that it becomes better adapted to the liturgical text. Examples of rhythmic and melodic changes, and of shifting the contrapuntal parts in relation to each other, are found interspersed with examples of direct quotations. Often good declamation of the words or expression of the text appears to guide the composer in choosing the material from the model. As shown in Ex. 21, Monte works exceptionally carefully in his adaptation of material from Giaches de Wert's madrigal *Cara la vita mia* (*a*) for the Credo of his Mass of the same name (*b*). Even considerations of a symbolic nature sometimes play a role in the choice of material.

EX. 21

(a)

in tan – to tem – po si tur-bat'e fie – ro

(b)

Fi – li –um De – i   u –ni-ge – ni-tum. Et   ex Pa-tre na-tum

EX. 22

Fortuna desperata

Kyrie

Kyrie

Kyrie

Kyrie

Ockeghem, Josquin, and Obrecht were among the Netherlanders who used parody at an early stage. Obrecht based his *Missa Fortuna desperata* on a model by Antoine Busnois; Ex. 22 shows the first bars of Kyrie II and of the model. This technique was used with increasing frequency by Clemens non Papa, Crecquillon, Gombert, George de la Hèle, Lasso, and Monte. In their Mass compositions one encounters a repertoire of chansons, German Lieder, madrigals, and motets, pieces which enjoyed great popularity in the sixteenth century. Together these composers compiled, as it were, a rich anthology, showing through their reworking of earlier music that they wished to pay tribute to previous composers, in many cases those who had already died. When the same model was adapted many times an element of competition was clearly also present.

3

Sacred Music as a Symbolic Language

NOWADAYS the sacred music of Netherlands composers is generally appreciated from a primarily aesthetic point of view. Yet it is worth considering that such an approach may largely represent a misunderstanding of its essential' character and purpose. If one wishes to understand something of its original meaning, one must concentrate on the original function of this music. In this case we must try and put ourselves in the situation in which the music originated, and to transport ourselves to the church building where it was performed. In doing this the distance of five centuries must be bridged: since the Renaissance we have recognized music as one of the fine arts, and the appreciation of music has developed in such a way that the expression 'art for art's sake' is now employed. For Netherlands composers, however, the warning of the Parisian master builder Jean Mignot (*d c.*1410) was still valid: 'Art without science is nothing'.[1]

In the fifteenth and sixteenth centuries the functions of worship and of music within worship were interwoven. Sacred music derived from worship, in the most comprehensive sense, its own terms of reference; that is, it had its place in an existing system of understanding and belief, a system that formed the composer's psychic reality. Anyone who stands outside this reality will not find it easy to grasp the essential character of Netherlands polyphony, since it was written to take its place within an existing system of understanding and belief.

THE CATHEDRAL

In a certain sense a comparison may be made with the significance that a religious building, especially a cathedral, had for Christians. The cathedral must in fact be seen as the product of a highly sophisticated building technique which was determined not only by mysticism, but also by the scientific observation of nature, in order to bring about a visionary

---

[1] See C. Jacq, *Le message des constructeurs de cathédrales* (Monaco, 1980), 63.

representation of the world to come. 'The cathedral is a magical interpretation of the cosmos ... the only manifestation of the medieval creative genius in which all of its contradictions are reconciled, the spiritual and the material, the natural and the grotesque, science and magic, devotion to Christ and devotion to the Virgin Mary.'[2] Since the notion of the cosmos was too great for men to grasp, the cathedral had to symbolize it in a manner such as the eye and the mind could encompass.

The cathedral was therefore first and foremost a representation of the heavenly Jerusalem, following the vision of St John as described in Revelation: 'I saw the holy city, and the new Jerusalem, coming down from God out of heaven, as beautiful as a bride all dressed for her husband' (Revelation 21: 2). According to the Byzantine scholar Photius, 'the betrothed arrives in the sanctuary, just as if he had entered heaven itself'.[3]

The idea of the cathedral as a consecrated city, a holy mountain, had its origins in the Near East. The city stands on a holy mountain (Psalm 48: 2) where God will meet his people (Exodus 19: 11). The ascent of the steps which lie at the foot of the cathedral can be seen as climbing the mountain in order to behold God: 'In the days to come the mountain of the Temple of Yahweh shall tower above the mountains and be lifted higher than the hills. All the nations will stream to it ...' (Isaiah 2: 2). A cathedral is therefore never high enough: it towers above the entire city, and on its buttresses there are images which cannot be distinguished from below. Is the prophecy of Isaiah being depicted here?

The cathedral is the *civitas Dei*, God's Kingdom, in stone, reflecting the architectural ambitions shown by medieval man in the Low Countries. After he experienced the reality of climbing mountains on his pilgrimages to Santiago de Compostela, Rome, and Jerusalem, the similarity between his church and a mountain must have come to his mind. Thus, the fundamental rule for the symbolic interpretation of church architecture is that its form was determined more by its symbolic worth than by its function. The rule seems also frequently to have applied in the interpretation of sacred music. Just as in the eyes of medieval man good and evil spirits inhabited the summits of mountains, so representations of saints and grotesques adorned the cathedral (see Fig. 13). Similarly, manuscripts of music intended for the cathedral often contain strange figures (see Fig. 14).

---

[2] P. Fingesten, 'Topographical and Anatomical Aspects of the Gothic Cathedral', *Journal of Aesthetics and Art Criticism*, 20 (1961), 3. Some other thoughts in the introduction to this chapter are taken from this article.

[3] See G. Bandmann, *Mittelalterliche Architektur als Bedeutungsträger* (6th edn., Berlin, 1979), 66.

FIG. 12. The Cathedral of Rheims, drawn by Eugène Viollet-le-Duc in his *Dictionnaire raisonné de l'architecture française du xiᵉ au xviᵉ siècle* (Paris, 1854–68). The earthly church imitates the heavenly one; her worship gives man the feeling of belonging to another world.

FIG. 13. One of the ninety-six figures on the flying buttresses at St John's Church in 's-Hertogenbosch. These images, erected at the beginning of the sixteenth century, combine to form a grotesque world. Perhaps the masons allowed themselves to be inspired by the concept of a cathedral as the City of God (see Figs. 14 and 19).

Music formed an essential part of the liturgical services held in church. It had to raise the liturgical texts above the spoken word and adorn the worship. When the word 'worship' is understood—as in Thomas Aquinas—as bringing to God the praise due to him, it is clear how important the role of musician was. He must have been conscious of the fact that liturgy was a holy event, a 'holy exchange' whereby 'God . . . sanctifies man and the thus sanctified man turns to God with prayers and offerings'.[4] Christian worship takes place entirely in the framework of expressive acts; it is essentially linked to symbolism. Two elements are most important: word and gesture. We shall see how the symbolic language of church architecture and that of worship also inspired the Netherlands composer to use symbols in his music.

SYMBOLISM IN NOTATION

The most simple and direct form of musical symbolism is certainly that of notation. About 1430 black and red notation began to make way for so-called white mensural notation, in which notes foreign to the metre were indicated in black. In this way the composer was given the opportunity to draw attention to words associated, literally or figuratively, with darkness or death by the use of black notes. Thus Jacob Obrecht chose black notation for the words 'sepultus est' in the Credo of his *Missa Schoen Lief*: the reference to burial emphasized the idea of Christ's death. A similar example may be found in the works of Josquin; in the Gloria of his *Missa De beata virgine*, the words 'Qui tollis peccata mundi' (That takest away the sins of the world) are coloured in each voice. The idea of sin as a hindrance in achieving sanctity holds a central place in the last Agnus Dei of the Mass. In this text, 'Lamb of God, that takest away the sins of the world, grant us peace' , which in the fifteenth century was sung during the kiss of peace, the Christian implores God to grant peace as the answer to his sins. Antoine de Févin expressed this thought in a beautiful way in his *Missa Mente tota*: the superius and bass are written entirely in white notes, and the alto and tenor all in black. Thus the colours in the choirbook appear diagonally, so that they too symbolize the crucifixion of Christ. Sometimes the colour black was used more literally, for instance in a passage from Lasso's four-part Requiem, where the words 'obscura tenebrarum loca' (the dark place of the night) in the Offertory are expressed visually for the singer.

---

[4] *Liturgisch Woordenboek*, ii (Roermond, 1965–8), col. 1573.

FIG. 14. The Kyrie from the *Missa Au travail suis* by Johannes Ockeghem, in the Chigi Codex. The manuscript was prepared in the studio of the Dutch copyist Petrus Alamire (see also Fig. 3). Before he settled in Antwerp in 1503, Alamire was active in 's-Hertogenbosch. The grotesque figures which appear so often in the margins of his choirbooks, and typify the work of his studio in Antwerp and later in Malines, were

possibly inspired by the paintings of Jeroen Bosch, who was a fellow townsman. Perhaps the fantastic beasts on the buttresses of St John's Church in 's-Hertogenbosch (see Fig. 13) were also influenced by the painter. Rome, Biblioteca Apostolica Vaticana, Chigi C. VIII. 234.

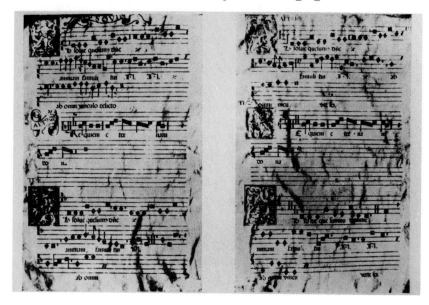

FIG. 15. The motet *Absolve, quaesumus Domine* by Josquin des Prez. Toledo Cathedral, Biblioteca capitolar, Ms. 21.

No composer has used black notation as a symbol of mourning in a more penetrating manner than Josquin. He wrote his five-part lament on the death of the aged master Ockeghem completely in black notation, and again used this symbolic form of notation in his prayer for Obrecht, who died in 1505:[5] 'Release, we pray, the soul of your servant [Jacob] from all chains of sin . . .'. The impression which the notation of the *Absolve* must have made on the contemporary musicians who sang this text is scarcely imaginable (see Fig. 15).

Apart from the colour of the notes, the composer had other means at his disposal. For instance, Josquin notated the superius part of the Sanctus of his *Missa Gaudeamus* as shown in Ex. 23. The circle, the notational symbol for triple metre, appears three times, emphasizing the word 'holy' in a profound sense: the number three has from antiquity been considered to be the number of holiness.

[5] See W. Elders, 'Josquin's "Absolve, quaesumus, domine": A Tribute to Obrecht?', *Tijdschrift van de Vereniging voor Nederlandse Muziekgeschiedenis*, 37 (1987), 14–24.

EX. 23

Sanctus

THE SYMBOLISM OF
THE *CANTUS PRIUS FACTUS*

It was mentioned above that church architecture in the Middle Ages had more to do with its symbolic value than with its function; the same is true for the basic structure of many Masses and motets. This is particularly the case for Mass cycles based on a *cantus prius factus*. In the previous chapter it was stated that the tenor, the part which generally presents the *cantus prius factus*, is the voice on which all others are based. The comparison that Johannes Grocheo makes with the foundations of a building is therefore particularly apt in this context. The form which the composer adopted for the individual parts of his Mass was naturally determined largely by the melodic shape of the *cantus prius factus*. One might now expect that a melody which served as a starting-point for a newly composed Mass was selected in accordance with its function in the *Kyriale*, but Netherlanders very seldom made use of this possibility. They turned more frequently to the wider repertoire of chant in general, or even to secular songs, in order to choose a melody, the original text of which could lend deeper meaning to the composition.

As a first example of this we may mention Johannes Regis's *Missa Dum sacrum mysterium*. The tropes added to the Mass text suggest that this work was composed in honour of the Archangel Michael. Already in the Kyrie there is an insertion, 'Dum sacrum mysterium cerneret Johannes Archangelus Michael tuba cecinit', a text taken from the Magnificat antiphon for his feast-day. Michael appears in the Bible as the protector of the Israelites (Daniel 12: 1) and leader of the angels in the fight against the devil (Revelation 12: 7); in the Middle Ages he was above all the patron of the Church. From the fourteenth century his name was mentioned in the 'Confiteor' at Mass directly after those of God and Mary. From the fourth century onwards holy places were erected in the name of the angel, and later a strong devotion to Michael developed, with pilgrimages to the ninth-century Mont St Michel in Brittany among other places. Above all, castle churches were dedicated to Michael, such as the Castel Sant'Angelo in Rome. It is not surprising that the symbolism of mountains played an important role here too. Strangely enough, in the Kyrie the text 'Dum

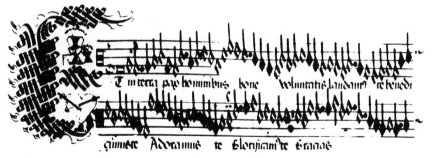

F IG. 16. Fragment from the Gloria of the *Missa O Venus banth* by Gaspar van Weerbecke. The initial at the beginning of the alto part shows a heart pierced by two arrows, which is a symbol of two lovers. The song on which the Mass is based suggests that it may have been for a nuptial Mass: 'O bond of Venus, o burning fire. How much that fine, pleasing woman now controls my heart!' Venus's bond means that the relationship must be permanent. Rome, Biblioteca Apostolica Vaticana, Cappella Sistina, Codex 51.

magnum mysterium' is set not to the appropriate antiphon chant but to the melody of the song 'L'homme armé' (see Ex. 1). The text of this reads:

> L'homme, l'homme, l'homme armé,
> L'homme armé doibt on doubter.
> On a fait partout crier
> Que chascun se viegne armer
> D'un haubregon de fer.
> L'homme, l'homme, l'homme armé,
> L'homme armé doibt on doubter.

(Have respect for the armed man. Everywhere there are cries that everyone must clothe himself in a coat of mail.)

The song dates from the second half of the fifteenth century, and probably came into existence shortly after the fall of Constantinople, possibly at the instigation of the Order of the Golden Fleece, which consisted entirely of 'armed men'.[6] Western Europe saw itself to be threatened by a Turkish invasion and prepared for battle (see p. 97). The polytextual chanson *Il sera pour vous conbatu | L'ome armé*, possibly by Antoine Busnois,[7] even mentions the 'dreaded Turk'. Constantinople had become a centre for the veneration of the archangel since the Emperor Constantine had

---

[6] See W. F. Prizer, 'Music and Ceremonial in the Low Countries: Philip the Fair and the Order of the Golden Fleece', *Early Music History*, 5 (1985), 128.

[7] In his article 'Antoine Busnoys and the l'Homme armé Tradition', *Journal of the American Musicological Society*, 39 (1986), 288–93, R. Taruskin gives arguments for ascribing the chanson *Il sera pour vous conbatu | L'ome armé* to Busnois.

built a great basilica there in his honour: there were more than thirty churches dedicated to him in the city. It can easily be supposed that Regis wished in his Mass to direct a prayer to Michael, who so clearly had 'deserted' the Eastern Church to defend the Church of Rome against the Turks. In view of the fact that the disputed articles concerning the Holy Spirit are omitted—as a gesture of reconciliation to Constantinople—in many early 'L'homme armé' Masses, these compositions can perhaps in a more general sense be counted as 'sacred battle songs'. Even in the seventeenth century, days of prayer were held in Antwerp for the protection of Western Christendom from the Turkish threat.

In this context the 'Caput' Masses mentioned above require an explanation. Three Masses carry this title: recent researches have shown that one work published under the name of Dufay may in fact be English, and there are also compositions by Ockeghem and Obrecht. The history of the origins of these works shows the strong influence that the symbolic language of the Church could exercise on the form of a Mass composition. While a *cantus prius factus* Mass was normally based on a complete song, the composers of 'Caput' Masses limited themselves to a single melisma, namely the melodic cadential formula associated with the word *caput* in the antiphon 'Venit ad Petrum'. The antiphon text concentrates on the dialogue between Peter and Christ on the occasion of the washing of feet during the Last Supper (John 13: 6–9), in which Peter says, 'Then, Lord, [wash] not only my feet, but my hands and my head [*caput*] as well!' Only the final word, *caput*, was employed. There are various possible reasons why this particular melisma was taken as the point of departure for Mass cycles. It has been suggested the Masses were intended for use on Maundy Thursday, when the celebrant was a bishop (otherwise no Gloria would have been allowed). Another occasion for their use could have been the coronation of a Pope; in this case the symbolism lies in the reference to Peter as *caput ecclesiae*, the first primate of the Church. But the debate over who was the real head of the Church, the Pope or the council, also gives an acceptable explanation for the composition of the first 'Caput' Mass. Particularly under Eugenius IV (1431–47), this problem occupied minds during the Council of Basle of 1431–9.

ARCHITECTURE, MORAL PHILOSOPHY, AND MUSIC

Besides Mass cycles, there are also many motets whose forms have symbolic meanings. Numbers, used in various ways, often seem to have been a guide for the composer in the conception of his works. But there are also examples of motets in which the composer realized ideals of contemporary architecture, and of buildings which took account of musical principles.[8]

Among the early works of Guillaume Dufay there are a number of ceremonial motets which are constructed according to the principle of the Golden Section.[9] The four-part motet *Vasilissa, ergo gaude* gives a clear example of this method; it was written in about 1420, perhaps for the engagement of Cleofe Malatesta and Theodorus Palaiologos, the son of the Byzantine Emperor. The structure of the motet is isoperiodic (see p. 34): after a freely composed, two-part vocal introduction (lasting eight longas) the tenor enters with the Gradual from the Mass for a virgin who has not suffered martyrdom: 'Concupivit rex decorem tuum' (The king has greatly desired your beauty). The melody of the Gradual extends over two *taleae*, each of which is thirteen longas in length. The golden section is a mathematical relationship in which a line is divided into two unequal sections so that the ratio of the shorter to the longer is equal to that of the longer to the whole. From the Renaissance onwards this principle was held to be the *proportio divina* (divine proportion) by many theorists of architecture, and it was put forward as the basis for architectural design. The form of Dufay's motet can be represented by the following diagram:

```
    E.......................................................................................
    C...............................................................
                                         D .....................................
              B..........................................
    A.................
tenor: _____|_____|_____|
              talea I                          talea II
    (rests)   Concupivit rex . . .
```

Therefore $A:B = B:C$ (or $8:13 = 13:21$); and $D:C = C:E$ (or $13:21 = 21:34$).

It is possible that Dufay used this geometrical concept in order to acknowledge the Malatestas' love for harmonious relationships in archi-

---

[8] See, for example, R. Wittkower, *Architectural Principles*, 9: '. . . for Alberti—who follows here a tradition unbroken from classical times—music and geometry are fundamentally one and the same; that music is geometry translated into sound, and that in music the very same harmonies are audible which inform the geometry of the building.'

[9] See M. Sandresky, 'The Golden Section in Three Byzantine Motets of Dufay', *Journal of Music Theory*, 25 (1981), 291–306.

tecture. In 1446 the great Italian architect Leone Battista Alberti was commissioned by Sigismondo Malatesta to transform the Church of S Francesco in Rimini into the Tempio Malatestiano, using Pythagorean proportions.

In other compositions from the same period Dufay demonstrates that he was acquainted—as was Johannes Ciconia in Padua—with the humanist ways of thinking which defined intellectual life in Italy in the fifteenth century. This is evident in, among other things, the character of the texts which he used and the rhetorical principles according to which he formed his music. But the most striking expression of the ideas of humanism is found in Dufay's application of faux-bourdon technique (see p. 42).[10] It can be clearly demonstrated that the composer employed this remarkable chordal progression in two of his secular works under the influence of the revival of ancient Greek music theory. The treatise *De musica*, attributed to Plutarch, was particularly popular among musicians. Music also plays an important part in Plutarch's *Moralia*.[11] Basing his argument on Plato's *Timaeus*, Plutarch wrote that intervals, having similar properties, may result in a *symphonia* which is pleasing to the ear, 'Since the consonant relationships all owe their existence to defined numerical relationships'.[12] The numerical relationships which were accepted as appropriate for harmony are the fourth (4 : 3), fifth (3 : 2), octave (2 : 1), twelfth (3 : 1), and fifteenth (4 : 1). The concept of *harmonia* is closely connected to that of *symphonia*. Plutarch was responsible mainly for working out the harmonic numerical relationships. According to him *harmonia* is an ideal, a model which shows man how he can arrive at a harmonious equilibrium and a peaceful frame of mind. In his *Moralia* he often makes a connection between musical harmony and the harmonious conduct of one's life, taking friendship and marriage as examples. It was not for nothing that the humanists allowed themselves to learn from this concept, for their ideal was in fact to educate men in morality so that they would live harmoniously.

Of the consonant intervals named by Plutarch as creating musical harmony, the fourth was the only one which was allowed to be used in parallel motion according to fifteenth-century musical theory. Given that the stereotyped character of a passage in faux-bourdon unavoidably

---

[10] See W. Elders, 'Humanism and Music in the Early Renaissance', *Report of the Twelfth Congress of the IMS, Berkeley 1977* (Kassel, 1981), 883–7.

[11] See J. Smits, *Plutarchus en de Griekse muziek* (Bilthoven, 1970).

[12] *Plutarch Moralia*, with an Eng. trans. by F. C. Babbit (London and Cambridge, Mass., 1959), 389 D.

brought with it a certain monotony, it is clear that this style was probably utilized for extra-musical reasons.

Dufay's earliest faux-bourdon composition is the Communion *Vos qui secuti estis me* from the *Missa Sancti Jacobi*. The complete text of the prayer reads: 'You who have followed me will sit on thrones to judge the twelve tribes of Israel'. These lines, taken from Matthew 19: 28, close the passage about the rich youth. The moral of Christ's words is that anyone who wishes to be perfect must give his possessions to the poor and follow him. The Apostle James the Great, for whose feast the Mass was written, had followed Christ unconditionally. By introducing the principle of faux-bourdon in the closing part of the Mass, Dufay was suggesting that the middle (third) voice was 'unconditionally' following the upper voice a fourth lower (see Ex. 18). In medieval Christian writings and iconography, the apostles who followed Christ were compared with bees that followed their 'king'. Since in French the term *faux bourdon* was applied to a drone, the earliest use of faux-bourdon technique appears to have a symbolic significance.[13]

There are also short passages of faux-bourdon in Dufay's motet *Supremum est mortalibus bonum* (see p. 34). This composition, written for the celebration of a peace treaty, offers a convincing illustration of the use of parallel fourths to symbolize in musical harmony the idea of friendship. Though originally they faced each other as enemies, Eugenius IV and Sigismund have now met as friends. It opens with the words, 'The supreme good for mortals is peace, the best gift from the highest God' (see Ex. 24).

In Plutarch's *Moralia* the unity of man and woman in marriage is also compared to two consonant notes, which create unity despite their difference in pitch.[14] It is striking, then, that Dufay, who was a bachelor in canon law, set a text which treated the problem of divorce, and that in places where the indissolubility of marriage was mentioned he used faux-bourdon technique. The first part of this text, 'Juvenis qui puellam', was familiar as a legal argument from the twelfth century.

MUSIC TO SYMBOLIZE THE MOTHER OF GOD

Since we have seen in the case of the Archangel Michael how strongly the composer could be inspired by devotion to the saints, we may now

---

[13] For a full account of the evidence, see W. Elders, 'Guillaume Dufay's Concept of Faux-bourdon', *Revue belge de musicologie*, 43 (1989), 173–95.

[14] *Moralia*, 139 D.

EX. 24

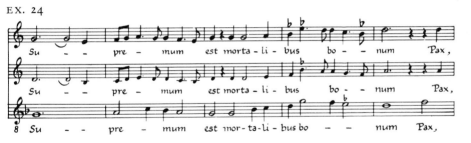

consider a theme which held a central place in the music of the
Netherlanders. This theme is the cult of Mary. More compositions were
dedicated to her during the Renaissance period than to any other saint,
and the symbolism connected with the Holy Virgin influenced many
composers to adopt very striking musical structures.

Mary won a place in poetry through poets such as Dante and Petrarch,
and she came to be viewed as a woman of uncommon beauty and the
patroness of the highest human gifts. In France and the Netherlands great
cathedrals erected in her honour were described as 'palaces of the Queen
of Heaven', and as such were depicted in a splendid manner by Jan van
Eyck and others (see, for example, van Eyck's *Madonna in the Church*, now
in the Staatliche Museen in Berlin). In the Royal Portal of Chartres
Cathedral the seven liberal arts are depicted doing homage to her.
Devotion to Mary reached a high point in the new Age of Chivalry under
the dukes of Burgundy. Despite the fact that ecclesiastical scholars held a
different opinion, in the eyes of many the Virgin became equal to her Son;
whenever she asked him a favour it was granted. The outcome was obvious: in the words of Chaucer, Mary was an 'Almighty and all-merciable
Queen'. In a period during which Netherlands painters interpreted the
Last Judgement and the terrors of hell in such an unusually visionary
manner, sinful man turned again and again to the *Mater misericordiae*.
Occasionally she was even blackmailed.[15]

The earliest setting of Petrarch's canzone *Vergine bella*, in which the
sinner glorifies Mary, is by Dufay. The aspects described above of the
humble relationship of prayer between poet or musician and the Heavenly
Queen receive a refined musical expression. While the words 'miseria
estrema' (the utter misery) lie in the lowest tessitura of the vocal parts, the

15 See G. Ashe, *The Virgin* (London, 1976), 220.

EX. 25

A - ve,   pec - ca - to - rum   mi - se - re - re.

closing words 'e tu del ciel regina' (and you, Queen of Heaven) are set as an all-overarching jubilus.

In the same composer's antiphon *Alma redemptoris mater*, the words which best honour Mary are supplied with lengthy melismas: *alma* (mild, blessed, sublime), *stella maris* (star of the sea), and *virgo* (virgin). As in Petrarch's canzone, weak mankind asks her help in the closing line of the text. At this very place Dufay adopts a new musical style, consisting of chords prolonged with pauses which forcefully command attention (see Ex. 25).

Already in the first centuries of Christianity the way to heaven was portrayed as a ladder, the *scala regni coelesti*. The motifs of Jacob's ladder and of the ladder of virtue are frequently found in early Christian art. Dante writes in his *Divine Comedy*: 'Within the crystal . . . I saw . . . a ladder set up, so far above, my eyes could not follow it'.[16] According to the theologian Fulgentius of Ruspe (468–532) Mary herself 'has become a ladder to heaven, since God through her descended to earth and men through her may ascend to heaven'.[17] Ten centuries later the ladder motif still played an important role in theological writings and in art. Around 1475 Domenico Benivieni's study *La scala della vita spirituale sopra il nome di Maria* appeared (see Fig. 17). Leonardo da Vinci and Filippo Lippi also used the ladder symbolism, and composers were not left behind.

In the first tenor of his five-part Marian motet *Virgo coelesti* Loyset Compère used the hymn melody of the same name, which was also one of the melodies sung to 'Ut queant laxis', the hymn made so famous in the history of notation by Guido d'Arezzo. The middle voice sings only the hexachord ut–re–mi–fa–sol–la, which is heard three times, on each occasion in smaller note-values. The rising line of the melody unquestionably recalls the ladder along which the musicians, as servants of Mary, wish to climb to heaven (see Ex. 26).

When the first theological study of Mary, the *Compassion de Marie* by Michel François, appeared in Lille towards the end of the fifteenth

[16] *Paradiso*, xxi. 25–30.

[17] See G. Heinz-Mohr, *Lexikon der Symbole. Bilder und Zeichen der christlichen Kunst* (4th edn., Düsseldorf, 1976), 185.

FIG. 17. The ladder which leads to the heaveniy city. *Intellectus* ascends the scale of creation, the steps of which are labelled: stones, flame, plant, brute, man, heaven, angel, and God; they lead from the lowest states of being to the highest. Woodcut in the *Liber de ascensu et descensu intellectus* by Raymundus Lullus (Valencia, 1512), which describes the stages the intellect passes on its journey towards the understanding of all being.

century, there was a fast-growing devotion to Our Lady of the Seven Sorrows. The example of St Saviour's Church in Bruges was followed in many churches, and Mary was depicted pierced by the *septem dolores*, or 'seven sorrows'. Adriaan Isenbrant, for instance, painted a madonna for the Church of Our Lady in Bruges: she is seated on a Renaissance throne, and on either side of her and above her head are seven scenes, each representing an individual sorrow.[18]

---

[18] See W. Elders, *Studien zur Symbolik in der Musik der alten Niederländer* (Bilthoven, 1968), 108 f. Isenbrandt's painting is reproduced as Fig. 6 in this book.

EX. 26

SYMBOLIC SEVEN-PART WRITING

There is scarcely a closer connection between this type of Marian devotion and music than that seen in the motet *Memorare mater Christi* by Matthaeus Pipelare. The text of this hymn deals with the *mater dolorosa*. The motet is written for seven voices, and each is called 'dolor' (sorrow) in the only surviving manuscript of the piece: 'Primus dolor', 'Secundus dolor', and so on. In the miniature embellishing the manuscript the Madonna is depicted in a blue robe embroidered with gold, while behind her back seven swords are hidden. The *cantus prius factus* is written with red ink in the 'Tertius dolor': 'Nunca fue pena mayor' (Never was sorrow greater), a *canción* written by Pipelare's compatriot Johannes Wreede in about 1470 on a text by his patron, the first Duke of Alva. One of the most famous music manuscripts of the Spanish court, the *Cancionero de Palacio*, opens with this composition.

It is not certain whether Pipelare's motet or Jacob Obrecht's *Missa Sub tuum praesidium* is the earliest example of seven-part writing in the history of the Netherlands School. Neither is it known whether Obrecht wrote his Mass in Bruges or Antwerp. In any case the number seven affected the structure of this Mass cycle in two ways. It begins with a three-part Kyrie, and in each new section the composer adds an extra voice, so that the seven-part Agnus Dei is a symbolic apotheosis. But the number seven is also present in another sense: apart from the antiphon 'Sub tuum praesidium', which is heard like a chorale melody in the superius in each of the five sections of the Mass (see Ex. 7), Obrecht included another six Marian chants in the work. Regis's *Missa Ecce ancilla Domini* and Gombert's motet *Salve regina* are also structured according to this prin-

FIG. 18. Mary as mother of the seven sorrows. The inscription 'Sicut lilium inter spinas' (As a lily among thorns) is taken from the Song of Songs, Woodcut, Antwerp, 1519.

ciple. Gombert's piece bears the appropriate designation 'Diversi diversa orant' (Various voices pray with various texts).

Until about 1550 seven-part composition was a seldom-used scoring. Of the 1,387 compositions published between 1543 and 1561 by Tielman Susato, fifty-three are for six voices, eight for eight, and only one for seven—this is by Jheronimus Vinders (see p. 69). The works of Clemens non Papa prove most clearly that seven voices were used almost exclusively for symbolic purposes. There is only one seven-part composition in his *œuvre* of about 230 motets: this is *Ego flos campi*, written in 1550 for the Illustre Lieve Vrouwe Broederschap during his time in 's-Hertogenbosch. The text is taken from the Song of Songs (2: 1–2; 4: 15), and its theme is devotion to Mary. Clemens underscored the words 'sicut lilium inter spinas' (as a lily among thorns), the motto of the confraternity, using homophonic chords, thereby combining praise of the Virgin with that of the brotherhood. The same text was set, also for seven voices, by Andreas Pevernage in 1577; it was dedicated to the Archbishop of Cambrai and included in the collection *Cantiones sacrae*.

There are also seven-part Marian motets among the works of Adrian Willaert and Philippe de Monte. Willaert included five seven-part motets in his collection *Musica nova* of 1559, among them the sequences *Benedicta es, coelorum regina* and *Inviolata, integra et casta es Maria*. Monte published a cycle of Marian motets in 1589 in which he not only used the number seven vertically in the scoring, but also expressed it horizontally by dividing the cycle into seven parts. As his text he took the 'Hymnus ad Dei param virginem', the concluding item in a monumental study of the Virgin by the Netherlands doctor of the Church Peter Canisius, which was published in Ingolstadt in 1577. It is notable that Canisius's hymn has twenty-two verses, and that Monte has omitted the second of these so that the remaining twenty-one verses can be divided evenly between the seven *partes* of his cycle.

There are some parody Masses in honour of the Virgin where the original scoring of the model is changed for the sake of number symbolism. These Masses take their musical material from two particularly popular six-part motets by Josquin, *Benedicta es, coelorum regina* and *Praeter rerum seriem*. George de la Hèle's choirbook of 1578, which was published by Plantin, contains eight Masses; the two final works are based on these motets by Josquin, and in the process of parody a seventh voice has been added in both. More than twenty years earlier Cypriano de Rore had used the same principle in his Mass on *Praeter rerum seriem*; it is his only Mass for seven voices, and the full texture is regularly reduced to five, four, or even three voices in the course of the composition, not only for short passages but also in complete sections. This indicates that he used seven-part writing to conform with an idea rather than because of any purely musical considerations.

The number seven, as a symbol of the sorrows of Mary, became a number which symbolized sorrow or mourning in general during the fifteenth and sixteenth centuries. There are, for example, motets for martyrs scored for seven voices, such as *Salve Barbara martyr* by Pierre

Moulu and *Sancte Stephane* by Pierre de Villiers. Similarly, when the mourning concerned a deceased prince, the composer sometimes employed seven-part writing as a means of expression. The seven-part *Proch dolor*, an anonymous motet which may possibly be attributed to Josquin, was probably performed during the period of mourning for Emperor Maximilian I, which took place on 27 and 28 February 1519 in Malines. After the death of Emperor Ferdinand I in 1564, his court composer, Johannes de Cleve, wrote the seven-part *Austria Danubii*. In both compositions chant from the liturgy of the dead forms the basis for the polyphony.

In this connection it might not be surprising to learn that Netherlands composers also symbolized their mourning for their departed fellow musicians in seven-part laments. This too can be illustrated by two examples. The Flemish composer Jheronimus Vinders wrote a *Lamentatio super morte Josquin de Prés*, based on two chants from the Office for the Dead. The piece begins eloquently with the words 'O mors inevitabilis, mors amara, mors crudelis, Josquin des Prés dum necasti ...' (O inevitable death, bitter death, cruel death, to take the life of Josquin ...); this text also forms the epitaph on a portrait of the composer which was placed above an altar in the choir of St Gudule's Church in Brussels after his death. The second musician remembered in a seven-part lament was Jacobus Vaet, whose pupil Jacob Regnart set the text *Defunctum charites Vaetem ...*: 'By sorrow [overcome] the Graces seek the dead Vaet ...'.

It was undoubtedly due to such compositions that the number seven remained a common symbol of sorrow until late in the Renaissance. One of the finest testimonies to this are John Dowland's seven *Lachrimae* pavans, which he called the 'Seven Teares'.

THE *REMISSIO PECCATORUM*

Medieval number theory, incidentally, ascribed many meanings to the number seven, not least because it frequently appears in the Bible to express totality, in both a positive and negative manner. For example, one speaks of the seven cardinal virtues, the seven cardinal sins, and the sevenfold graces. Cassiodorus named seven forms of the forgiveness of sins, possibly referring to the following text in Matthew 18: 21–2: 'Then Peter went up to him and said, "Lord, how often must I forgive my brother if he wrongs me? As often as seven times?" Jesus answered, "Not seven, I tell you, but seventy-seven times."'' There is no doubt that

EX. 27

Johannes Ghiselin was inspired by this thought when he repeated the same motif of a fourth seven times in the bassus at the article 'I acknowledge one baptism for the remission of sins' in the Credo of his *Missa Je nay dedeul* (see Ex. 27). Shortly before, Tinctoris had even stated in his treatise on counterpoint that a composer may not repeat any motif unless he does it with some special intention.

For the same reason Guillaume Dufay based his Gloria *De Quaremiaux* on a short cantus firmus, which appears seven times in the bass. The character of the melody is reminiscent of the ringing of bells. The work was almost certainly composed for the liturgy of the Easter vigil, in which after the forty-day fast the Gloria is heard once again and bells are rung as a sign that the time of penitence is over. The French word *caresme* or *carême* (Lent) is recognizable in the title. Through the sevenfold present-ation of the cantus firmus, the composer expresses the hope that the sins of man may be forgiven through fasting.

TRINITAS IN UNITATE

When mensural notation (in which the length of the individual notes was measured) began to come into use in about 1250, theoretical terms such as *modus perfectus* and *tempus perfectum* were introduced. The word *perfectus* in this context means that the note-length in question can be divided in three; thus it comprises 'beginning, middle, and end'. The circle, a sign without beginning, middle, or end, appeared as a symbol for this rhythmic pattern. This is no surprise, since triple metre was associated with the Trinity, the Three in One and the eternal perfection.

Various compositions prove that the Netherlanders were inspired by this symbolism of the Trinity. And it was natural that they should adopt the canon as a means of expression: indeed, in its most simple form the circular canon (as it were, without an end), written for three voices notated in one part, is an almost ideal symbol of the idea of 'one God in three Persons'.

One of the earliest examples can be found in the works of Antoine Busnois. The only known source of his canon *Ha que ville* is a chanson in which the motto 'Trinus in unitate' appears above the superius. The meaning of the motto becomes clear when the superius is isolated from the two lower parts, and this part is performed as a three-part canon at the unison. It is not impossible that Busnois adapted the canonic part into a chanson only later, and then dedicated it to Jacqueline d'Hacqueville (see p. 99).

The most famous example of a Trinity canon is the Agnus Dei II from Josquin's *Missa L'homme armé super voces musicales* (see p. 39). The brilliant use of counterpoint in this canon undoubtedly inspired later composers to employ similar devices: there is a three-part canon with the motto 'Trinitas in unitate' in the Agnus Dei of George de la Hèle's parody Mass based on Josquin's sequence *Benedicta es*, and Palestrina wrote a three-part canon under the same motto in the Agnus Dei of his *Missa ad fugam*.

There are also passages in the motet repertoire which contain the sign of the Holy Trinity. The text of the first part of the motet *Pater de coelis* by Pierre de la Rue reads as follows:

> Pater de coelis, Deus, miserere nobis.
> Fili redemptor mundi, Deus, miserere nobis.
> Spiritus sancte, Deus, miserere nobis.
> Sancta trinitas, unus Deus, miserere nobis.
>
> Heavenly Father, God, have mercy on us.
> Son, redeemer of the world, have mercy on us.
> Holy Spirit, have mercy on us.
> Holy Trinity, one God, have mercy on us.

Three of the six parts of the composition form a canon, which is clearly deliberate. The same composer also conceived his four-part motet *Laudate Dominum* as a canon 'three in one'; its text consists of Psalm 116, to which an extra line concerning the Trinity is added.

Finally, there is an example from the works of Heinrich Isaac. His motet *Angeli archangeli* finishes with the line 'Beata Trinitas unus Deus'. At the entry of these words the six-part writing gives way to a three-voice texture (superius I, alto, and tenor II); the same words are subsequently answered by superius II, tenor I, and bass, as it were in a heavenly antiphony.

MUSICA COELESTIS

Ockeghem had already realized, in a masterly canon, the technique hinted at in Isaac's Angel Motet. His thirty-six-part *Deo gratias* is conceived for four nine-part choirs. What can we grasp from the score of such an extraordinary piece? Each choir sings its own canon, consisting of a melody which is invariably imitated at the unison. Just before the first voice in the first choir reaches its thirty-bar long (!) closing note, the first voice of the second choir enters. The canon melody of the third choir is twice as long as that of choirs 1 and 2. The result is that voices 19–36 are taking part in the polyphony at the end of the piece, while voices 1–18 are holding the closing note. The choice of four nine-part choirs for a composition bearing the title *Deo gratias* cannot have been arbitrary. The number four perhaps symbolizes the four winds of heaven; these played an important role in the construction of churches, and even in the liturgy. The number nine certainly denotes the nine ranks of angels, who also have a place in the liturgy. According to this notion, Ockeghem's *Deo gratias* is a heavenly song of praise, performed in antiphony between the nine choirs of angels and from all points of the compass to the praise of God. The composition of this piece as a circle canon shows the unending nature of the song of praise. The composer was also familiar with this concept, for the text of the Mass contains these words at the end of the Preface: 'And therefore with Angels and Archangels, with Thrones and Dominations and with all the host of the heavenly army we sing the hymn of thy glory, evermore saying...'. The following lines were written about Ockeghem's canon by the poet Nicolle le Vestu more than twenty-five years after the composer's death:

> Ung facteur fut Okghem nommé,
> Roy sur tous chantres renommé,
> Qui faist en des pars trente six
> Ung motet tellement assis
>
> There was an artist named Ockeghem,
> King of singers, very famous,
> Who composed in thirty-six parts
> A motet with such choruses

Only a negative answer may be given to the question of whether this giant canon was ever in fact performed in Ockeghem's time. The composition has survived without text, and any attempt to set the words 'Deo gratias' satisfactorily to the music fails. A more important argument, however, concerns the ideal context in which we should consider the 'motet'. For

FIG. 19. One of the nineteen musicians on the flying buttresses of St John's Church in 's-Hertogenbosch. The viola da gamba shown here is just one of the various percussion, wind, and plucked and bowed stringed instruments (see also Fig. 13).

the fifteenth-century composer, music was placed at the service of the Creator: his work was a *laudatio Dei* (glorification of God). In the fine arts too there are eloquent testimonies to this attitude. The images on the flying buttresses of St John's Church in 's-Hertogenbosch provide an example: the ninety-six stone figures are extremely high up, and cannot be distinguished from the ground (see Fig. 19). Perhaps the sculptors who created this set in the beginning of the sixteenth century were inspired by Psalm 96. Honorius of Autun, when referring to this psalm, factorized the number ninety-six into twelve (the teaching of the twelve apostles) and eight (the teaching of the eight beatitudes).[19] The ninety-six figures are divided into two groups of 8 × (6 + 6) on either side of the nave of the church.

It is less simple to explain why Josquin also conceived his psalm *Qui habitat in adjutorio Altissimi* for four choirs, each of which sings its own six-part canon. Clearly, Ockeghem's *Deo gratias* provided his model. The compositional process is in fact the same, though Josquin exceeds his 'teacher': he allows not eighteen but twenty-four parts to develop into an impressive polyphonic complex. The number twenty-four may point to the twenty-four elders of the apocalypse (Revelation 4: 4), who according to Adam of Fulda sing the praise of God together with the angels. On the other hand, wherever Josquin allows the basic compositional numbers, four and six, to function symbolically it is better to think of the number four as a sign of the creation of the cosmos, and the number six as a sign of the creation of the *sexta creatura*, man. Looked at in this manner, his canon is a song of praise from man and the whole cosmos to God.

The small *œuvre* of Ghiselin Danckerts includes a particularly remarkable composition which perhaps also belongs to the category of heavenly music. It is a puzzle canon on the text 'Ave maris stella', a well-known hymn in honour of Mary. Danckerts conceived four parts which can be combined with each other rhythmically and harmonically in twenty different ways.[20] As the musical 'units' are notated in the squares of a chess-board, the musician must attempt to discover a solution or solutions by moving them. The canon was printed in 1549 by Melchior Kriesstein in Augsburg (see Fig. 20), and is also included in *El melopeo* by the Spanish theorist Pietro Cerone, which appeared in 1613 in Naples. Some exponents of rhetoric in the Low Countries also devised puzzle poems in the form of a chess-board.

Picture motets are the final example of *musica coelestis* to require our attention here. These are a unique phenomenon in music history, dating from the last twenty years of the sixteenth century. Artist, engraver, and composer co-operated to create a religious image, which included a polyphonic motet written specially for this purpose. The composer gave

---

[19] See H. Meyer, *Die Zahlenallegorese im Mittelalter. Methode und Gebrauch* (Munich, 1975), 175.

[20] See H. Westgeest, 'Ghiselin Danckerts' "Ave Maris stella": The Riddle Canon Solved', *Tijdschrift van de Vereniging voor Nederlandse Muziekgeschiedenis*, 36 (1986), 66–79.

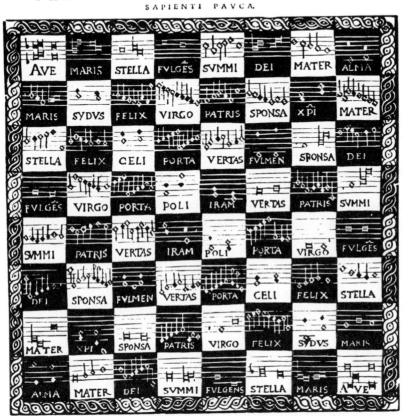

GHISILINVS DANCKERTS,
QVATVOR VOCVM,
VNIO.

CANON.

QVOD APPOSITVM EST. ET APPONETVR.
PER VERBVM DEI BENEDICETVR·
SAPIENTI PAVCA.

FIG. 20. The Marian hymn *Ave maris stella* by Ghiselin Danckerts. This four-part puzzle canon, notated in the form of a chess-board, can be solved in twenty different ways. The composition was printed in Augsburg in 1549. Wolfenbüttel, Herzog August Bibliothek.

the artist his music; the artist copied it note for note into his painting, and the engraver transferred the representation on to a copper plate, from which prints were eventually made. The centre of the art of creating picture motets was Antwerp. One of the engravings shows the announcement of Christ's birth to the shepherds; Andreas Pevernage composed a nine-part *Gloria in excelsis* which was incorporated into a painting by Martijn de Vos, and Jan Sadeler manufactured an engraving from this picture (see Fig. 21). The fact that a complete composition can be represented in such a small format in this collaborative art-form may appear amazing, yet the musician would soon have been struck by the ideal aspect of such artistic expression. Again he had a composition before him which was conceived not for a performance in this world,[21] but purely as an imitation of what the composer imagined to be the song of praise of the nine choirs of angels.

'GEMATRIA'

When Luca Pacioli published his *De divina proportione* in 1509 he announced on the title-page that his study was intended for those who practised philosophy, perspective, art, sculpture, architecture, music, and other mathematical subjects. Writing in his *Compendium musices* about half a century later, Adrianus Petit Coclico divided composers into four categories. The second consisted of 'mathematici' (see Fig. 22). This scientific classification was undoubtedly an outcome of one of the methods frequently employed by composers. It was above all the Netherlanders who, with extreme ingenuity conceived numerical structures as the basis for their compositions. Certainly a composer had a specific intention in using these mathematical concepts. But in a period which saw brotherhoods for the initiated, secret sects, rites, and symbols, it was assumed that such numerical structures should be esoteric. The music historian who wishes to uncover the structures has a difficult task. Sometimes, however, he may have a stroke of luck, and what he then discovers can only increase his respect for the technical ability of these composers. Often the principle of 'gematria' was applied; this is a method of exegesis employed by medieval cabalists in which letters are converted into numerical values. Various alphabets can, depending on the text, serve as the starting-point: the Hebrew, the Greek, and the Latin. When the Latin alphabet is used gematrically the letter a has the value one, b has the value two, and so on. The letters i and j, and u and v are indicated by the numbers nine and twenty respectively.

---

[21] This naturally does not mean that the motet could not have been sung. There is a recording of it (*Gloria in excelsis Deo*, Christoforus-Schallplatte SCGLB 75966), in which it is repeated to disguise its short duration.

FIG. 21. The announcement of Christ's birth to the shepherds. The angels hold music paper, on which the nine parts of Andreas Pevernage's *Gloria in excelsis* are written. The image was engraved in Antwerp by Jan Sadeler after a painting by Martijn de Vos (Antwerp, 1587).

An early example of gematric composition can be found in the works of Johannes Tinctoris.[22] As music teacher to Beatrice of Aragon in Naples he was involved in the compilation of a beautifully illuminated chanson album dedicated to the princess (see p. 142). He is moreover the only

(see p. 142)

---

[22] See J. van Benthem, 'Concerning Johannes Tinctoris and the Preparation of the Princess's Chansonnier', *Tijdschrift van de Vereniging voor Nederlandse Muziekgeschiedenis*, 32 (1982), 24–9.

DE MVSICES
Definitione.

Vsica secundum Iosquinum, est recte, &
ornate canendi atçp componendi ratio.
Continet enim hæc ars regulas & præce-
ptiones,quæ pueris uiam tradunt ut recte,
& suauiter canant præscriptam contilenam,& ut ip-
simet artificiose componant cantus atçp Symphoni-
as,Nec pro Musico habendus est,qui non in utroqp
hoc officio Musices excellit, aut aliquid egregij pre-
stare possit. Verum paulo post in partitione eorum,
quæ hic docenda sunt , quàm late pateat huius artis
usus obiter ostendemus , & dabimus operam ut in
exemplis,& usu canendi pueros diutius,quàm in præ
ceptis detineamus.

DE MVSICORVM
Generibus.

Pero me operæ præcium facturum,si obi
ter meum, de uarijs Musicis iudicium o-
stendam.Non enim omnes pari in re præ
stantes fuerunt : Quisçp in eo excelluit,
ad quod pertingere potuit. Ideo hæc non scribo, ut
uel minimo omnium aliquid detraham, sed ut ado-
lescentes ex me discant iudicare de his Musicis,qui lo
gè ante nos exstiterunt,uel etiam hodie in uiuis sunt.

Inuenio autem quatuor Musicorum genera.
Primum genus eorum est, qui primi Musicam in-
uenerunt, & uarijs in rebus uocum quandam Har-
moniam obseruarunt,Quorum primus Tubal He-
bræus

bræus. Lamech filius fuisse fertur, quem alij postea
secuti sunt, & inuentis semper aliquid addiderunt,
ut Anphion,Orpheus, Boetius, Guido Arenen-
sis,Ockghem, Iacobus Obrecht, Alexander,& alij
multi,quorum etiam scripta hunc in diem extant, hi
autem tantum Theorici fuerunt.

Secundum genus, est eorum qui sunt Mathematici,quorum compositiones, nemo est, qui non
ferat.At hi ueru Musices finem non sunt assequuti.
Nam etsi huius artis uim intelligunt, & etiam com-
ponunt,non tamen ornant suauitatem, & dulcedi-
nem cantus,& quod peius est,cum uellent artem in-
uentam latius propagare,& illustriorem reddere,de
nigrarunt eam potius, & obscurarunt. In docendis
enim præceptis & speculatione nimis diu manent,et
multitudine signorum,& alijs rebus accumulandis,
multas difficultates afferunt,& diu atçp multum di-
sceptantes, nunquam ad ueram canendi rationem
perueniunt. Ex quibus sunt, Io. Geyslin,Io.Tin-
ctoris,Franchinus,Dufay,Busnoe, Buchoi,Caron-
te,& conplures alij.

In tertio genere,sunt Musici præstantissimi, &
ceterorum quasi reges, qui non in arte docenda
hærent, sed theoriam optime & docte cum pra-
ctica coniungunt, qui cantuum uirtutes, & omnes compositionum neruos intelligunt, & uere sci-
unt cantilenas ornare, in ipsis omnes omnium affe-
ctus exprimere,& quod in Musico summum est, &
elegan-

FIG. 22. The *Compendium musices* by Adrianus Petit Coclico, published in Nuremberg in 1552. On the pages reproduced above Coclico discusses the four categories of musicians; the second group consists of mathematicians. (See also Fig. 2.)

composer to be represented by two short motets on Latin texts in this collection (which otherwise contains secular music): *O Virgo, miserere mei* and *Virgo Dei throno digna*. According to the heading the first is dedicated to Beatrice. The composer honours 'Beatrice of Aragonia' by using the numerical value of her name, namely 133, to determine the number of notes in the superius part:

B	e	a	t	r	i	c	e		d	e		A	r	a	g	o	n	i	a
2	5	1	19	17	9	3	5		4	5		1	17	1	7	14	13	9	1 = 133

He signs the composition with the 121 notes (representing Tinctoris) of the lowest part, the countertenor:

T	i	n	c	t	o	r	i	s
19	9	13	3	19	14	17	9	18 = 121

In bars 8 and 9 of the motet the word *miserere* appears in all three parts in a striking section of black notation: the twenty-one black notes possibly allude by means of the numbers two and one to the letters B and A.

Jacob Obrecht also employed gematria to address a prayer directly to God in a personal way.[23] His three-part *Parce Domine* contains forty-four words of text and the same number of bars. Following the cabalistic tradition, this number represents the name of God written out in Hebrew letters: JHWH. The forty-four words together contain ninety-seven syllables. This number gematrically denotes the name Jacob Obrecht:

J	a	c	o	b	O	b	r	e	c	h	t		
9	1	3	14	2	14	2	17	5	3	8	19	=	97

Furthermore, the composer also clearly determined the total number of notes in his motet, using a scheme which he had previously calculated exactly. In the first section there are forty-four notes, in the third eighty-eight, and in the middle section 121. Thus while Obrecht names Jahweh twice in the music, he signifies by the use of the number 121 (11×11) that he has transgressed against the law (namely, the Ten Commandments) and asks forgiveness for his sins. Perhaps the total number of notes should also be symbolically interpreted: $44 + 121 + 88 = 253$. The number 253 may be factorized into twenty-three and eleven. In the number twenty-three, the sum of the numbers nine and fourteen, the initials J and O can be recognized, and the number eleven functions once again as a symbol of sin.

The composer on whose gematric constructions the most research has been done is Josquin. In several of his compositions the shape of the tenor part, which forms the basis of the music, proves to be dictated by a number which is the sum of a row of figures, each of which signifies a letter. The letters then reveal a name.

The use of mensuration canons in Ockeghem's *Missa Prolationum* and Josquin's *Missa L'homme armé super voces musicales* was discussed in the previous chapter, but more light must now be cast on the relationship between these two compositions. Only then shall we be able to understand why Josquin wished to honour Ockeghem in his Mass. One cannot doubt that the *Missa Prolationum* was the 'father' of Josquin's composition, given the exceptional character of the contrapuntal technique and the younger composer's acquaintance with the work of the older master. Though Josquin reserves his cleverest specimen of proportional canonic writing for the final section of the Mass, he immediately presents, in each of the three sections of the Kyrie, a two-part mensuration canon: in Kyrie

[23] See. K. Vellekoop, 'Zusammenhänge zwischen Text und Zahl in der Kompositionsart Jacob Obrechts. Analyse der Motette "Parce Domine"', *Tijdschrift van de Vereniging voor Nederlandse Muziekgeschiedenis*, 20 (1967), 97–119.

Signature of Johannes Ockeghem

1 between tenor and superius; in the Christe between tenor and alto; and in Kyrie 11 between tenor and bass. The note-values of the 'L'homme armé' melody which provides the material for these canons are in a relationship of 2 : 1, 4 : 1, and 3 : 1 in the three sections respectively. However, Josquin uses the well-known 'L'homme armé' melody (see Ex. 1) in a different version, which, not surprisingly, was never employed elsewhere: it is presented in each of the five sections of the Mass in the same form, comprising exactly sixty-four notes. When Ockeghem's name is written out in the spelling he used in his signature, the sum is sixty-four:[24]

$$O \quad c \quad k \quad e \quad g \quad h \quad e \quad m$$
$$14 \quad 3 \quad 10 \quad 5 \quad 7 \quad 8 \quad 5 \quad 12 \; = \; 64$$

Perhaps it is no accident that the bass of Kyrie 11 contains ninety-nine notes; this number is the numerical value of the Christian name of the composer of the Mass (see below). If these notes really signify the name 'Josquin', the part counts as his signature.

A convincing example of a gematric signature in a composition which Josquin dedicated to Mary is provided in his motet *Illibata Dei virgo*. One might call this work a musical self-portrait for a variety of reasons. Several prominent motifs are found elsewhere in Josquin's *œuvre*. The text is a song of praise to Mary, 'the immaculate virgin and mother of God', but at the same time it forms an acrostic which reveals the name of the composer.[25] However, Josquin goes further than creating a textual bond between his name and that of Mary: one of the five parts consists of an

[24] D. Heikamp published this discovery in his article 'Zur Struktur der Messe "L'omme armé super voces musicales" von Josquin Desprez', *Die Musikforschung*, 19 (1960), 121; however, the author takes his analyses so far that there is reason to doubt a number of his statements. Josquin also uses exactly 64 notes for the Latin closing words, 'Requiescat in pace. Amen', in his lament on the death of Ockeghem, *Nymphes des bois*. See J. van Benthem, 'Struktur, Zahl und Symbol in den Kompositionen von Johannes Ockeghem', *Musica antiqua. Acta scientifica* (Bydgoszcz, 1982), suppl. vol., 3.

[25] On this acrostic and its various solutions see W. Elders, 'Josquin des Prez en zijn motet "Illibata Dei virgo"', *Mens en Melodie*, 25 (1970), 141. The gematric treatment of Josquin's name that I discovered was further elaborated by J. van Benthem; see the article mentioned in ch. 5 n. 3, 36 f.

EX. 28

ostinato motif of the three notes la–mi–la (see Ex. 28). These notes, which are heard alternately on d^1 and on g, stand for the name Mary. This is revealed in the second verse at the line 'Consola "la mi la" canentes in tua laude' (Comfort those who sing 'la mi la' to your honour). The spelling of the composer's name in the acrostic yields the following figures gematrically:

J	o	s	q	u	i	n		d	e	s	P	r	e	z	
9	14	18	16	20	9	13	= 99	4	5	18	15	17	5	24	= 88

The 'la–mi–la' motif is heard twenty-nine times altogether in the tenor part. The number of ostinato notes is therefore eighty-seven. Although it would have been simple for Josquin to end the composition (in G Dorian) on the note g of the last statement of the ostinato, he adds another four bars and gives the tenor an extra d^1. The total number of ostinato notes is therefore brought up to eighty-eight. Though it is naturally not certain a priori that this number symbolizes the family name of the composer, there are indications in the structure of this part which support our hypothesis. As far as the tenor part is concerned, there is absolutely no sign of a mathematically consistent compositional method. On the contrary, in the first section of the motet the ostinato is heard only three times, and in the second section twenty-six times; such a structure is exceptional in Josquin's *œuvre*. However, the composer effects a certain measure of balance between the two sections since the motif is heard in perfect longas (very long note-values) in the first half. The initial of the Christian name Josquin has the numerical value of nine. While the composer therefore signs the entire tenor part with his family name, he places the initial of his Christian name in its first section. Moreover he recalls his complete Christian name in the line 'Consola "la mi la" canentes in tua laude': the four parts which surround the tenor consist of exactly ninety-nine notes and four 'la–mi–la' motifs.

A composition related to *Illibata Dei virgo* is Josquin's five-part *Salve regina*. In this Marian motet, too, the key to understanding the ideal plan of the text and music lies in an ostinato motif. The motet has three sections, in which the tenor part consists exclusively of the motif sol–fa–sol–ut, the first four notes of the chant 'Salve regina'; it appears

EX. 29

twelve times in the first section, four times in the second, and eight in the third. Once again the *soggetto ostinato* sounds alternately on g^1 and d^1, preceded each time by three bars' rest (see Ex. 29). Each presentation of the motif is therefore based on the Marian number seven. The alternating forms of the theme sol–fa–sol–ut constitute in total a series of twelve double 'Salves', or twenty-four single ones. This number must be seen as an explicit reference to the woman of the Apocalypse (Revelation 12: 1): 'Now a great sign appeared in heaven: a woman, adorned with the sun, standing on the moon, and with the twelve stars on her head for a crown.' (see Fig. 23). A contemporary of Josquin, the Master of the Antwerp Triptych, created a sensitive representation of the same text in his panel *Maria in de Zon.*[26] As in the motet discussed above, Josquin adds some notes to the tenor part in the closing cadences of the three sections of the *Salve regina*, namely one, one and two respectively. By this means he increases the number of notes ($24 \times 4 = 96$) to exactly one hundred. This total can be explained with the help of the direction found at the beginning of the tenor part: in most sources of the motet the motif is not continually repeated, but written out a few times and provided with the motto 'Qui perseveraverit (usque in finem, hic) salvus erit' (He who endures to the end will be saved). The musician must obviously have conceived this device as a reference to the text in the third section of the motet: 'Et Jesum, benedictum fructum ventris tui, nobis post hoc exsilium ostende' (And show us, after this our exile, Jesus, the blessed fruit of your womb). These words reveal to the faithful Christian the aim of his life. In the Greek name for Christ, χριστός, the initial letter is identical to the roman numeral X; the number ten therefore serves as a symbol for Jesus. This demonstrates a causal relationship between the meaning of the text and the total number of one hundred ($= 10 \times 10$) ostinato notes.

The compositions described above find their structural basis primarily in the principle of gematria. But some examples show that gematria can appear alongside other types of number symbolism. And sometimes the symbolic meaning of the numbers goes far beyond a 'simple' treatment of

---

[26] Now in the Boymans-van Beuningen Museum, Rotterdam.

FIG. 23. Albrecht Dürer, detail from a woodcut of the Woman of the Book of Revelation (1498).

the letter-values. Josquin's works include a Mass composition, the *Missa Gaudeamus*, based on a mystical number series, the individual parts of which can be meaningfully interpreted.[27] This composition, intended for the feast of All Saints, belongs to the large category of works of art which are determined in some way by the visions of St John described in the

---

[27] See W. Elders, 'Josquin's "Gaudeamus" Mass. A Case of Number Symbolism in Worship', *Studi musicali*, 14 (1985), 221–33, in which an extended treatment of this Mass is presented. An excellent explanation of the meaning of numbers in medieval thought may be found in Meyer, op. cit. (above, n. 19).

Book of Revelation. These include mosaics in Roman basilicas, stained-glass windows in Romanesque and Gothic churches, book illustrations by the Limbourg brothers, tapestries by Jan Bondol and Nicolas Bataille in Angers, woodcuts by Albrecht Dürer and Lucas Cranach, and the altar-piece by Hubert and Jan van Eyck in Ghent. It cannot be proved that Josquin ever had the opportunity to examine this last painting—one of the 'seven art wonders of Ghent'. But he did sing for years in the choir of the cathedral in Milan, where there is a stained-glass window by Stefano da Pandino depicting the Lamb of God (see Fig. 24).

The Mass uses the Introit of All Saints as its *cantus prius factus*. Even though the complete chant melody is included in the Mass, the main structural element is its opening motif, which Josquin treats in a most unusual manner. It is heard sixty-one times in all, and these motifs are divided extremely irregularly between the sections of the Mass, implying the presence of some deliberate fundamental scheme. The total of six statements in the Kyrie functions as a sign of the anticipation of salvation and refers, according to medieval belief, to the end of time: Christ's death took place on the sixth day, from the sixth hour, and thus men will be saved through the number six. Also man can be taken into the multitude of the saints through performing the six works of mercy. In the Gloria the motif is heard fourteen times; this number refers to the fourteen saints to whom one may turn for help in particular situations, and also serves as a multiple of seven, which symbolizes not only the seven deadly sins but also the seven gifts of the Holy Spirit, from which the seven cardinal virtues derive. The 'Gaudeamus' motif is heard only twice in the Credo, the longest of the five sections of the Mass. The confession of faith forms the basis of the two covenants: the old covenant was turned in to the new through the blood of Christ, and in the Credo the believer enters a personal covenant with God the Father. The superius of the Sanctus uses the motif three times in a high tessitura and long note-values, which make it reminiscent of the sound of a trumpet (see Ex. 23). At the same time the motif appears once in the alto and then in the tenor. The numbers three and two signify faith in the Trinity and action in accordance with the command to love God as well as man. In the song of praise 'Hosanna in excelsis' the motif is heard seven times. Here Josquin refers to Revelation 10: 7: 'At the time when the seventh angel is heard sounding his trumpet, God's secret intention will be fulfilled . . .', meaning that 'The all-embracing plan of God is to accomplish through Christ everlasting salvation and the total defeat of evil'.[28] In the Agnus Dei too the motifs are divided into two separate series. The text of the Agnus Dei is a prayer

FIG. 24. Stefano da Pandino, the Lamb of God and the Last Judgement. Stained-glass window in the choir of Milan Cathedral, *c*.1450. The words 'Et libri aperti sunt' (while the book of life was opened) are taken from Revelation 20: 12. The numerical structure of Josquin's *Missa Gaudeamus* is based on the visions described in this book.

to the Lamb of God, which takes a central place in so many apocalyptic works of art. In more than one sense, this section of the Mass acts as a 'peroration'. The motif is heard four times in Agnus I, and it is clear that here the number four functions as a symbol of the Cross and of salvation. Only in this light can the twenty-three (!) 'Gaudeamus' motifs of the final Agnus Dei be explained; according to Honorius of Autun, this is the number of signs of the cross which the priest makes during the canon of the Mass. The numbers ten and thirteen (10 + 3) represent the Ten Commandments and the relationship of the Old Testament (10) to the New Testament (3 = the knowledge of the Holy Trinity): the adoration of Christ by the three Magi on the thirteenth day after his birth means that the law is fulfilled for the three continents, Asia, Africa, and Europe. Thus by the symbolic use of numbers in his *Missa Gaudeamus* Josquin showed that he also saw the feast of All Saints as the end of the pilgrim journey of mankind.

[28] The Bible trans. from the original texts, Willibrord edn. (Boxtel, 1981), 1743.

4

Secular Music

SINCE the biography of Netherlands composers leads us so often to Italy, it is scarcely surprising that most of their secular works were written to Italian texts. The fifty Netherlanders whose names are included in the Appendix set about 4,000 texts between them, of which 54 per cent are in Italian, 37 per cent in French, and 5 per cent in German. The remaining 4 per cent are almost evenly divided between Dutch and Latin. As will be indicated further in the next chapter, it is sometimes difficult, above all with the repertoire of the period around 1500, to determine whether settings of songs are for a combination of voices and instruments or purely instrumental. The sources leave us rather uncertain, and the contemporary performance practice was very free. But the contribution of the Netherlanders to secular music was of inestimable importance, not only in its quantity, but also in its quality. In the pages which follow its importance will be demonstrated through just a small number of compositions, which nevertheless allow us to gain an impression of the nature of the texts and musical forms.

More than sacred music, secular music owes its unprecedented flowering to the emancipation of the middle classes after 1500. We can read something about the musical life in the house of a regent's family in Brussels in a French–Flemish conversation booklet which was written in about 1540 and reprinted in Dunkirk in 1623 under the title *Ghemeyne T'samenkoutinghe*.[1] After attending church, where they hear (among other things) a motet by Lupus Hellinck, the gentlemen have their midday meal at the house of Master Jacob vanden Dale, and afterwards they take up partbooks themselves:

MASTER JACOB. Now then, shall we have a song?
ROMBOUT. You have indeed said well, my lord.
MASTER JACOB. Willeken [the page], go and fetch my books.
WILLEKEN. Which books would you like to have, my lord?
MASTER JACOB. The books in four and three parts.

[1] See R. Lenaerts, *Het Nederlands polifonies lied in de zestiende eeuw* (Malines, 1933), 155. See also David Wulstan's quotations from an English adaptation of the same booklet in *Tudor Music* (London and Melbourne, 1985), 42 and 81.

LADY CATTELYNE. Pour [a drink] for Dierick, Pauwels.

PAUWELS. Which wine would you like Dierick?

DIERICK. Give me white.

MASTER JACOB. I have drunk red.

DIERICK. What has that to do with me? I prefer to drink white: I'll serve you, Rombout.

ROMBOUT. Drink it, I'll let you know.

MASTER JACOB. What keeps you, Willeken?

WILLEKEN. I could not find them, Sir.

MASTER JACOB. Give them to Antoni. Antoni will look for some good songs.

ANTONI. Sir, do you wish to hear a song in four parts?

MASTER JACOB. It is all the same to me: sing what you want.

ANTONI. Dierick shall sing the treble; if it is too high for you, the children will help you.

ROMBOUT. Give me the contrabass.

ANTONI. There now is the contrabass. I will sing the tenor.

DIERICK. Who will sing the contratenor?

YSAIAS. I shall do it.

. . .

MASTER JACOB. Sure, that is a good song. Who composed it?

ROMBOUT. I believe it was Gombert.

MASTER JACOB. Who is he?

ROMBOUT. He is the master of the choirboys of the emperor's chapel.

MASTER JACOB. Truly, it is a good song; and who composed the other one?

DIERICK. Johannes Lupi, the singing-master from Cambrai.

MASTER JACOB. It is also good; well, Ysaias, to your good health!

The great flowering of secular music in the sixteenth century was made possible through the development of music printing. When Ottaviano Petrucci began to sell the first music in printed form in Venice in 1501 (see Fig. 46), the composer gained the opportunity to reach a wider public. Business men in the Low Countries quickly capitalized on the possibilities of the new technique, and particularly in Antwerp and Louvain, music printing reached an unprecedented level. Nowadays one can still marvel at the fabulous mastery of the printer Plantin in the museum named after him in Antwerp.

However much the composer was stimulated by a love for music-making among the middle classes, the most interesting part of the repertoire owes its origins more to patronage. The dukes of Burgundy and Savoy, the regents of the Netherlands, the kings of France, the emperors of the German-Habsburg Empire, and the Italian dukes were great lovers of music. At their courts the Netherlanders could see how the the old saying came about: 'La poésie sans la musique est comme un moulin sans l'eau' (Poetry without music is like a mill without water).

FROM BALLATA TO *VILLANELLA*

When Johannes Ciconia settled in Padua in about 1400, Italy was already enjoying a refined tradition of song. Francesco Landini, one of the last Italian masters in this field, died in 1397. The traditional song forms, such as the madrigal, ballata, and caccia, lived on for a few decades, and were taken over by the Netherlanders. For instance, the text of the ballata *O rosa bella*, a love-song set to music by Ciconia, is ascribed to the Venetian Leonardo Giustiniani. The ballata begins with a *ripresa*, followed by two *piedi*; then comes the *volta* and finally the *ripresa* once more. The composer

Ex. 30

adapted himself to this formal pattern: in accordance with custom, he wrote music only for the refrain and the first two lines of the following verse. The music was repeated for the remainder of the lines according to the following scheme: A (*ripresa*); bb (*piedi*); a (*volta*); A (*ripresa*). Ciconia set the song for a singer and two melody instruments. There is a great expressive power in the rising reiterations of the melody at the words 'ay lasso me, dolente' (woe is me, I am exhausted by sorrow) and 'soccorrimi' (come to help me) (see Ex. 30). The same formal scheme was applied about 1421 by Hugo de Lantins in his marriage song for Cleofe Malatesta of Rimini and Theodorus Palaiologos (see p. 60). This has a splendid poetic text which tells the Byzantine prince that his empire, which formerly accommodated Helen of Troy, will now be occupied by an even more divine being, 'Cleophe de malatesti'.

The first Netherlander to set a poem by Petrarch was Guillaume Dufay, who chose the opening verse of the ten-part *Vergine* cycle (see p. 63). The text of Dufay's canzone, which he composed about 1430, comes from a collection of poetry dedicated to Laura, but it has a religious orientation none the less. In spite of this, however, this musical jewel foreshadows the true Petrarch cult of the sixteenth century, which culminated in the art of the madrigal. Dufay's setting of the text is through-composed, and the form of his song is thus particularly modern: not until a century later did this principle become common for music with Italian texts.

EX. 31

Fortuna desperata

The Netherlanders who wrote music on Italian texts at the beginning of the fifteenth century had a great respect for the character of the text, and thus literary humanism entered the field of music. The literary 'Fortuna' tradition, continued in the Renaissance by Dante, Petrarch, and Boccaccio, became a source of inspiration for the secular music of later Netherlanders (see p. 122). Musicologists find it remarkable that Antoine Busnois, one of the few Netherlanders who does not seem to have been to Italy, was the composer of an Italian song, *Fortuna desperata*, which was extremely popular about 1500 (see Ex. 22). But it should not be forgotten that under Charles the Bold, Busnois's patron, Italian culture had a great influence on Burgundian court life. Busnois's *Fortuna desperata* contains an accusation addressed to Fortune: 'Desperate, foul, accursed Fortune . . .'. The two upper voices of the three-part texture appear together or separately as a *cantus prius factus* in more than twenty other compositions. The idea behind this is one of artistic emulation and demonstration of skill. This is proved clearly in the versions by Alexander Agricola, Heinrich Isaac, Josquin, and Johannes Martini. Martini added three instrumental parts to Busnois's superius; these express in the melodic shape the unpredictable character of the goddess, who is symbolized by, among other things, the turning wheel (see Ex. 31 and Fig. 25).[2] No less than five different versions of *Fortuna desperata* by Isaac have survived. The most intriguing is the five-part version in the *Cancionero de Segovia*. Again the new parts are added to the superius. Two of these form a *soggetto ostinato* in which a sacred litany is presented: one voice invokes the saints, 'Sancte Petre, [Sancte Paule]' and so forth, and the other answers with 'ora pro nobis' (pray for us). Isaac's setting is exceeded in its number of voices by Agricola, who takes all the voices of Busnois's original and adds three new instrumental parts to them.

   [2] See D. Kämper, ' "Fortunae rota volvitur". Das Symbol des Schicksalrades in der spätmittelalterlichen Musik', *Miscellanea Mediaevalia*, viii (Berlin, 1971), 363.

FIG. 25. The wheel of Fortuna. Woodcut in Sebastian Brant, *Der Sotten Schip* (Antwerp, 1548). The text above the woodcut contains the warning that those in the highest place will be the first to fall.

In the last decades of the fifteenth century, several new forms of secular song originated in Italy. Florence under Lorenzo de' Medici was a city of great festivals and masquerades. During these festivities the guilds displayed themselves at their best, and loved to perform so-called *canti carnascialeschi*, simple homophonic songs in which they described their skills. There is no doubt that Agricola and Isaac wrote such songs during their time in Florence, but these were lost under Savonarola when he burned many secular manuscripts. The Netherlanders' superiority to the Florentine musicians is illustrated by a comparison of the settings of *Scaramella* by Loyset Compère and Josquin with similar anonymous songs: with their lively syncopated rhythms, Josquin's and Compère's settings are each a humorous parody of soldiers' habits. Another centre where a new type of secular music, the *frottola*, developed was Mantua. Here Italian composers found a patroness in Isabella d'Este. Josquin's *El grillo* takes a place of honour among the hundreds of *frottole* which have been preserved. The original way in which he portrays the singing of the thirsty cricket—whoever that might be—charms everyone who hears the song for the first time.

It is understandable that Netherlanders who spent the greatest part of their lives in Italy could influence musical life considerably. Consequently the history of the Italian madrigal tradition is closely linked with names such as Adrian Willaert, Cypriano de Rore, and Giaches de Wert. They worked in Ferrara, Venice, and Mantua, where this new vocal ensemble music, which originated in the 1520s, received the impulses which enabled it to hold its dominant place for almost a century. The great interest in Petrarch cultivated by the d'Este family raised the literary character of the madrigal from its very beginnings, in contrast with that of the *frottola*, and the favourite sixteenth-century poets, Ariosto, Guarini, and Tasso, all enjoyed the protection of the d'Este family.

Willaert's collection *Musica nova* contains twenty-five madrigals, of which only one is not based on Petrarch. The preface of the edition of 1559 shows that the music had 'been hidden from the world' for years. Perhaps a number of compositions dedicated to Alfonso II d'Este date from Willaert's time in Ferrara. The madrigals, for four to seven parts, exclusively use sonnets as their texts and are through-composed. The atmosphere of the poem and the meaning of individual words are thrown into clear relief by the vocal scoring and choice of harmony. The seven-part *Liete e pensose*, for instance, is a dialogue between the poet and the friends of his beloved Laura. The poet's questions and the women's answers are set for contrasting vocal groups, while the content of the text is crucial for the harmonic conception. The low voices ask why Laura is not with her friends as usual, and the high voices reply with the phrase shown in Ex. 32. The contrast between the words 'Liete siam' (We are happy) here and 'dogliose' (sorrowful) in the next line is expressed in the harmony. Willaert often gives his madrigals a declamatory character; in the *frottola*, on the other hand, the text was subordinated to the music (*poesia per musica*). The fact that the voices are treated as equal partners contributed to the popularity of madrigal singing among those singers who liked working as soloists as well as in ensembles.

Rore had published his first book of madrigals at the early age of 26, and the reprints that followed prove that it was very successful. Like his

EX. 32

teacher Willaert, Rore allowed the structures of his compositions to be influenced by the content rather than the form of the poetry. His most important means of interpreting the text is melody, supported by harmony: melismas have an expressive rather than an ornamental value; sudden changes in the mood of the poem are realized in the harmony, so that the music has an increasingly dramatic effect. Rore's way of using chromaticism showed the way for later Italian composers such as Gesualdo, Marenzio, and Monteverdi.

The madrigals of Jacquet de Berchem come from the same period; by far the largest number of his compositions are settings of texts by Ariosto. Ariosto's epic *Orlando furioso* enjoyed an unparalleled popularity, and it became a gold-mine for composers, like Petrarch's *Canzoniere*. Jacquet was among the first to dedicate a composition to the hero Orlando—an extensive musical publication in three volumes. He set ninety-one stanzas to music and gave his work the appropriate title *Capriccio*, reflecting the variety of its texts.

The madrigals of Jan Nasco also follow the literary taste of his time. Under the influence of Guarini's *Il pastor fido*, a new form of poetry, the pastorale, developed as a reaction to the serious tone of Petrarcan verse, and Nasco gives a fine example of this idyllic combination of poetry and music in his *Canzon di Rospi e Rossignuol*, a dialogue between Damon and Amaryllis. After the opening words of the shepherd, his beloved answers that the singing of the nightingale gives her a sense of being in paradise. On hearing this Damon lets the frogs croak as well. Naturally, the

EX. 33

Che   nè   ma — ri nè   fiu — — — — — — — mi,

EX. 34

Di   co-lor, di ca-lor,di mo-   to pri - vo Già mar-moin vi- staal mar-moil vi-soaf-fis —

Di   co-lor   di ca-lor,di mo-   to   pri - vo Già mar-moin vi - staal mar-moil vi - soaf-fis —

Di   co-lor di ca-lor, di mo-   to pri - vo Già mar-moin vi - staal mar-moil vi - soaf-fis —

Di co-lor,di ca-lor,di mo   — to   pri - vo Già mar-moin vi - staal mar-moil vi-soaf-fis —

Di   co-lor, di ca-lor,di mo-   to pri - vo Già mar-moin vi- staal mar-moil vi - soaf-fis —

composer did not miss the opportunity to imitate the animal noises in the music.

Even though no composer wrote as many madrigals as Monte, his contribution to this genre is seen by music historians as less important than that of Giaches de Wert. In his first madrigal books Wert still shows the influence of his teacher, Rore. But later, in his search for new means of expression, he introduces more and more elements of the concertato style, which are intended to reflect the content of the text as precisely as possible. The great vocal technique of the sopranos who sang in the *concerto delle donne* in Ferrara enabled him to write exceptionally difficult madrigals, which were beyond the scope of dilettantes. Ex. 33, taken from his five-part *Non è si denso velo*, shows how the flow of a river is portrayed in his music. This melody is treated contrapuntally in the various parts. In more dramatic texts, such as those from Tasso's *Gerusalemme liberata*, Wert readily uses the *parlando* technique: he allows the singers, as it were, to speak. The madrigal *Giunto alla tomba* has a chordal passage at the words 'deprived of colour, warmth, and movement, the face is already like marble', in which the low scoring gives the recited text a melancholy character (see Ex. 34). In this music, which was published in 1581, Wert anticipated the development of monody.

The musical history of the Low Countries shows that the madrigal had success far outside the Italian borders. In 1600 Cornelis Schuyt published the first of two collections of Italian madrigals in Leiden. One of the pieces is a paean to his birthplace and contains such eloquent lines as 'Illustre Leyda, o perla preciosa, Per lettre chiara, in arme valorosa' (Illustrious Leiden, o precious pearl, famed for your learning, skilful in arms). The style of the music is related to that which he had come to know in Italy. Surprisingly enough, Schuyt used texts by Tasso for seven of his madrigals.

The so-called *canzone villanesca alla napolitana*, or *villanella*, developed in Naples in about 1540 as a reaction against the serious madrigal. The English theorist Thomas Morley described this genre as 'A clownish music to a clownish matter.' Originally rustic subjects were central in this music, as in the pastorale, but it quickly broadened its scope to other subjects. The poems, in regional dialect, often included very humorous double meanings. The composers chose well-known folksongs as a starting-point, and quite frequently allowed themselves to use parallel fifths and octaves, forbidden in the pure polyphonic art, in order to imitate simple folk-music. It is notable that Willaert, a foreigner, was the first composer to introduce this genre to Venice in 1542, where it gained great popularity. Diverse subjects and dialects gave rise to various genre designations. Thus Lasso, who at the age of 23 had already published a collection of *Madrigali villanesche* in Antwerp after a visit to Naples, composed a volume containing *moresche*; a *moresca* is a satirical piece which features black slaves. This second collection includes also the famous *Matona mia cara* and the eight-part *Zanni! Piasi patro?* The latter is a dialogue between Pantalone, a Venetian merchant, and Zanni, his servant from Bergamo, both stock characters from the *commedia dell'arte*. Zanni is caught by his master drinking wine in the cellar. On being ordered to come upstairs the servant replies that he has lost the stopper of the vat. The answer to that is, 'Stick your nose in it.' Suddenly Zanni thinks he has found the stopper, but it proves to be a dog's turd. The master suggests that he should stop his mouth with it. The dialogue finally ends with a mutual 'Adio'.

Hubert Waelrant, an associate of the Antwerp music printer Jan de Laet, also favoured this form of 'light' music. In 1565 thirty such compositions of his were issued in Venice, and a number also survive in manuscript.

THE ART OF THE CHANSON

Although the word 'chanson' is mostly used to mean a song in general, it refers here exclusively to a polyphonic song with French text. Like Italian secular music, the chanson encompassed a great diversity of texts and musical forms. French was the mother tongue of a great number of composers from the Low Countries, and even composers for whom this was not the case readily used the language. Thus no songs by Sweelinck on Dutch texts are known, whereas settings by him of French and Italian verse are.

In the fifteenth-century chanson courtship was 'elevated to the height of a Rite'.[3] The atmosphere is often elegiac. The texts are written in a mannered rhetorical style, and each belongs to one of the so-called *formes fixes*, the forms of late medieval French poetry and music: ballade, virelai, bergerette, and rondeau. One of the distinguishing features of these forms is the use of refrains and the repetition of music for various verses. Charles d'Orléans, Alain Chartier, and Christine de Pisan were among the greatest poets after Guillaume de Machaut. Gilles Binchois, Guillaume Dufay, and Antoine Busnois, however, sometimes wrote the texts for their music themselves. Their chansons were generally in three parts; the text lies in the upper voice, and two accompanying instruments played contrapuntal lines. *Instruments bas* were preferred, soft-sounding instruments such as lute, fiddle, recorder, and harp.

One of the chansons of Binchois is based on a poem by Chartier, a *rondeau quatrain* (refrain and verse, each consisting of four lines). The text is rich in antitheses and metaphors:

> Tristre plaisir et douloureuse joie,
> Aspre doulceur, reconfort ennuyeulx.
> Ris en plourant, souvenir oblieux
> M'accompangent, combien qui seule soye.
>
> Sad pleasure and painful joy,
> Bitter sweetness, unpleasant comfort,
> A tearful laugh, a forgotten memory
> Keep me company, even if they leave me alone.

The superius enters with this refrain after a short instrumental introduction (see Ex. 35). Binchois's four-part *Filles à marier* shows that he could adopt other moods. In a lively interaction of imitative parts, the composer advises marriageable girls not to marry, for whenever jealousy rears its head love comes to an end.

The chansons of Dufay form a world in themselves, and courtly love plays a less prominent part in his works. Besides melancholy there is joy, for example over the New Year, friendship, or good wine. In *Ce moys de*

---

[3] J. Huizinga, *The Waning of the Middle Ages* (2nd edn., London, 1955), 109.

may (see Fig. 26) Dufay gives the three voices the following text in a dancing rhythm:

> Ce moys de may soyons lies et joyeus,
> Et de nos cuers ostons merancolye;
> Chantons, dansons, et menons chiere lye,
> Por despiter ces felons envieux.

> In this month of May, let us be joyful and happy,
> And banish melancholy from our hearts;
> Let us sing, dance, and make merry
> To spite those who envy us.

In the last verse the poet and composer ask their lovers not to deprive them of this chance.

EX. 35

Hé, compaignons is a drinking-song in which Dufay proposes a toast to various friends. This piece forms a sharp contrast with his four-part *Lamentacion de Constantinoble*, the only one of his four settings to survive (see Fig. 38). The *cantus prius factus* of the latter piece, a verse from the Lamentations of Jeremiah sung on a simple recitation tone, lies in the tenor. The upper voice carries a French text: 'O tres piteulx de tout espoir fontaine . . .' (O most merciful, source of all hope . . .). The composition was perhaps sung during the banquet held by Philip the Good in Lille in 1454 in connection with the fall of Constantinople. A chronicler wrote:

All boundaries of admissable luxury were completely surpassed here. At the end of the festivities the guests had a shocking surprise: an artificially constructed elephant entered, led by a giant, dressed a Turk. The amazement reached its height when the sides of the beast opened: out stepped a person, dressed as a beguine, miserable in appearance and demeanour, in ragged clothes. She raised her hands to heaven and recited mournful verses; from this one understood that she represented the expelled Church of Constantinople which implored help and rescue from the might of the Turks.[4]

---

[4] Translated from *De Vastberaden Ridder: Elf houtsneden 'Le Chevalier délibéré' van Olivier de la Marche-editie Schiedam 1498*, ed. E. de Beaumont (The Hague, 1968), 5.

FIG. 26. Miniature of the month of May by the Gebroeders of Limburg in the book of hours, the *Très riches heures* of Jean, Duke of Berry. The picture shows festively dressed courtiers riding in the Parisian countryside. It was traditional to go into the country on the first of May. Various chansons were dedicated to this subject, such as *Ce moys de may* by Guillaume Dufay, a dancing-song for a mixed vocal and instrumental ensemble. Since it was performed in the open air, a group of loud instruments (*alta*) was probably used for the accompaniment. Chantilly, Musée Condé. *Très riches heures* (*c.*1411–16).

However, the crusade which Philip wished to undertake against the Muslims never took place.

Composers of the next generation adhered to the same formal schemes but occasionally based their chansons on a folksong. In *L'autrier la pieça* Busnois even uses two at the same time. His music is almost always dedicated to a woman, for instance to Jacqueline d'Hacqueville, whose name appears in five texts. Busnois's bergerette *Ja que li ne* is ambiguous, for its first line can be read in two ways: 'Ja que li ne s'i attende' (Though he does not expect it) and 'Jaqueline si attende' (Let Jaqueline wait). Line 8 names the colours of the Hacqueville coat of arms: the poet wears a blue and white sleeve as a token of his love.[5]

About 1500 the style of the chanson changed. The form became freer, and consequently texts consisting of dialogue could be better expressed, while folksong was used as a basis ever more frequently. The *chanson rustique*, a counterpart of the *villanella*, gained in popularity. The first composers to work in this genre were Mathieu Gascongne and Antoine de Févin. Gascongne's *Si j'eusse Marion* recalls the medieval *pastourelles* in which the shepherd Robin and the young shepherdess Marion appear. His chansons obviously filled a need, for they remained in the repertoire for more than fifty years. Josquin too made an important contribution to this genre in his three-part *A l'ombre d'ung buissonnet au matinet*; Ex. 36 shows how he arranged the folksong in this work. In some six-part chansons by Josquin, for example *Petite camusette*, the folksong, treated as a two-part canon, forms the backbone of the composition. Dutch folksongs were sometimes adapted in this manner, as can be seen in Josquin's *Entrée suis en grant pensée* and in *Par vous je suis* by Johannes Prioris. Both compositions are based on the love-song 'In mynen zyn haddic vercooren een meysken al soe jonck van jaren' (In my mind I had chosen a girl so young in years).

5 See *The Mellon Chansonnier*, ed. L. Perkins and H. Garey, ii (New Haven, 1979), 243.

This song was so popular that Cornelis Anthoniszoon painted it in his *Braspenningmaaltijd* of 1533.[6]

The late chansons of Josquin evoke a melancholy atmosphere; five of them contain the keyword 'regretz'. The best-known is *Mille regretz*, a favourite composition of Charles V. The chansons of Pierre de la Rue, which include the same word, probably originated at the court of Charles's aunt, Margaret of Austria. This music mirrors the unfortunate happenings in the life of the regent; in *Secretz regretz* the poet says, 'Secret sorrows, enemies of nature, have changed my joyful thoughts into mourning and suffering through painful torments'.

The name of Johannes Lupi, 'the singing-master from Cambrai', is mentioned in the scene from the conversation booklet quoted above (see p. 87). Perhaps he was still living when Master Jacob and his circle sang a 'good song' by him. Given that no songs by him on Dutch texts have survived, it is probable that one of his chansons was performed. After the red and white wine, his four-part *O vin en vigne* would certainly have been appreciated. This chanson was published in 1540 by Pierre Attaingnant of Paris, but it must of course have been in circulation for some time already by that date.

In the middle of the sixteenth century the most popular composer in the Netherlands was Thomas Crecquillon. No one else had more chansons published, either in their vocal versions or in arrangements for lute or keyboard. His choice of texts extends through all available subjects. When about 1550, a painter copied the *Concert in het ei* by Jeroen Bosch,[7] he symbolized lewdness with, among other things, a chanson by Crecquillon: 'Toutes les nuicts que sans vous je me couche . . .' (Each night that I go to bed without you . . .).

Amor seems to have dominated the lives of some in religious orders as well, and this point is wittily elaborated by Lasso and Gombert. Lasso has a priest make love to a nun; when the abbess who catches them asks what is going on, she receives the answer that the priest and nun were entangled as prisoners in a rosary. The composer underlines the humour of this moment by recalling the chants of the Lord's Prayer and Hail Mary. Nicolas Gombert places the following words in the mouth of a nun:

> Alleluya my fault chanter
> Quatre fois la sepmaine
> Le tard coucher lever matin

---

[6] This painting is now in the Historisch Museum, Amsterdam.
[7] Copy now in the Musée des Beaux-Arts, Lille.

Mon Dieu que cest grand peine.
La la ... sol fa my re
Plus ny seray nonnette
Ie accompliray toutes mes voluntez
Amours et amourettes.
La sol fa my re ...

I must sing Alleluia
Four times a week,
Late to bed and rising early
My God, that makes me tired.
La la ... sol fa mi re
If I were no longer a nun
I would fulfil my wishes
With affairs large and small
La sol fa mi re ...

Few composers have sung of the erotic so overtly as Clemens non Papa. His chanson *Frais et gaillard* emphasizes the high point of sexual delight in both text and music, and so can easily be counted among the genre of the *priapée*, a song in honour of Priapos:

Frais et gaillard ung iour entre cent mille
Je m'entre pris de faire ample ouverture
Au cabinet d'une mignonne fille
Pour accomplir les oeuvres de nature.
La fille my respond tel est mon appetit,
Mais mon amy je crains de l'avoir trop petit.
Quant elle me sentit s'escria notre dame:
Et tost, tost, tost, despeche vous, car je me pasme.

Hale and hearty, one day in a lifetime,
I took it upon myself to court openly
In the chamber of a sweet girl
In order to accomplish the works of nature.
The girl responded to me, 'I certainly have the desire,
But, my friend, I fear it's too small for you.'
But when she felt me, our lady cried:
Up, up, hurry up, because I am in raptures.

Composers also wrote songs which poked fun at an individual. Pierre de Manchicourt depicted the dialogue between Alis and Collette in a lively, declamatory style: when you are unlucky with your man, the most appropriate action is to 'put him to sleep', and to take a new friend. Jan Pieterszoon Sweelinck gave new life to an epigram by Clément Marot,

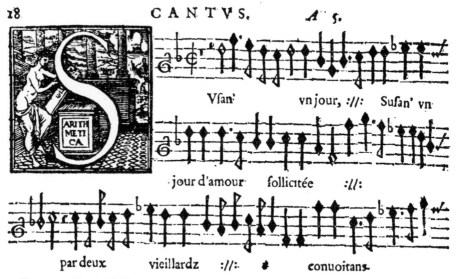

FIG. 27. The initial letter and first lines of the superius of the chanson *Susan' un jour* by Jacobus Vredeman. The song appears in a collection of secular music by Vredeman which was printed in 1602 by Giulio Radeo in Franeker. Among other works, the collection contains some polyphonic songs with Frisian texts. The Hague, Gemeentemuseum.

previously set by the French composer Janequin. *De Jan, Jan* describes the man who possesses everything that one can desire—except his wife. The name Jan was frequently used at that time as a nickname for a deceived partner in marriage.

The love for music cherished by the half-deaf poet Pierre de Ronsard certainly contributed to the attraction that many composers felt to his poetry. His *Les Amours de Cassandre* (1552) was published with an appendix of printed music containing settings by his contemporaries of ten of his poems, and some of these settings provide the music for all the other sonnets in the volume. At the end of the sixteenth century about 200 of his poems had been set, by over thirty composers. In *Comme la tourterelle* the poet describes how his heart languishes like a turtle-dove when he is not with his beloved. The gloomy atmosphere is reminiscent of the poetry of Petrarch, and it is therefore no surprise that Lasso, in his five-part setting of the poem, expresses this mood by means of chromaticism. In this way his chanson almost acquires the character of a madrigal. The more conservative composer Philippus de Monte set the same text to music; the splendid melodic lines in the five-part polyphony of this work compensate amply for the lack of up-to-date features.

Arrangements are the final aspect of the art of the chanson to be considered here. In 1544 Tielman Susato issued an edition of two- and three-part chansons, presenting simplified versions of original four-part pieces. One can describe these works as favourite pieces in a new guise. The preface to the collection shows that the printer had didactic intentions: if the inexperienced amateur sings the songs first in a small group, he will later manage better in a large group. However, there was sometimes also an element of competition in the arranging of chansons of older masters. This was particularly true of Gombert, who, for example, arranged two four-part chansons by Josquin for six voices. In the case of *En l'ombre d'ung buissonnet*, a different setting from that named above, he managed to make Josquin's double canon into a triple one by adding a third two-part canon to the original two. Of course, the quality of the original composition was not always improved by such arrangements. The saying 'De gustibus non est disputandum' (There is no accounting for tastes) obviously holds true for some musicians of the sixteenth century too.

LATIN SECULAR MUSIC

In 1552 eleven Latin comedies were printed in Utrecht; the author was Georgius Macropedius, or Joris van Lankveld, who was born about 1475 in Gemert. Remarkably enough, the author also wrote music for a choir, which enters at the end of the acts. Even if at first sight it may seem strange to encounter secular music with Latin texts, this may be explained by the background of humanism and the renewed interest in classical literature: one of the fruits of humanism was the definitive form which Renaissance Latin took about 1450.

The most important category of secular compositions on Latin texts consists of motets for particular occasions. Hundreds of motets have survived with humanistic Latin poems for their texts. It is often difficult to determine if the character of such a composition is sacred or profane. These types were combined if the text and music were written to mark the death of an important person, but of course pure secular ceremonial music also exists, for example in Dufay's motet *Vasilissa, ergo gaude* (see p. 60).

Antoine Busnois honoured his senior colleague Ockeghem with a motet when they were both staying in Tours in about 1465. The first section of the motet is dedicated to Pythagoras, the philosopher who defined the relationships of musical intervals. The second section opens with the words 'Haec Okeghem, qui cunctis praecinis Galliarum in regis aula . . .', which translates, 'Ockeghem, you who are foremost among the singers in the Royal court of France', and goes on: 'once entering upon the inheritance of these ancient implements as something to be practised by your offspring, you introduced them in the fatherland of Burgundy'.[8] Then the composer of the motet describes himself as the 'unworthy musician of the illustrious Charles the Bold'. One of the four parts is a *soggetto ostinato*: a motif of three notes (re–ut–re) is repeated a number of times at the intervals of the fourth, fifth, and octave, evidently because the relationships between these intervals were defined by Pythagoras.

A motet by Jacobus Vaet from the middle of the sixteenth century, *Stat felix domus Austriae*, pays homage to the Austrian royal house. Here too a *soggetto ostinato* forms the basis of the compositon, albeit one of a totally different shape: la–re–mi–sol–ut–fa–mi–re. It is thus a *soggetto cavato* (see p. 37).

Apart from humanistic Latin texts, the Netherlanders occasionally set texts by classical writers. Adrian Willaert was inspired to undertake his chromatic experiment *Quid non ebrietas* by the fifth letter of Horace. In this letter Horace invites his Roman friend Torquatus to visit him in the country one day to enjoy the good life and some wine: 'What a miracle cannot the winecup work! It unlocks secrets, bids hopes be fulfilled, thrusts the coward into the field, takes the load from anxious hearts, teaches new arts. The flowing bowl—whom has it not made eloquent?'[9] Willaert designs for this text forty bars of music in which the hexachords are mutated to the point that the musician progresses via double flats through the entire circle of fifths, an unprecedented device in this period. Just as Erasmus had written to Thomas More some years previously that his *Praise of Folly* was 'not wholly foolish', so Willaert could have said on completing this ode to wine that it was not composed in complete drunkenness.[10]

No lines of classical literature held such a great attraction for composers as the lament of Dido from Virgil's *Aeneid*. The first polyphonic settings of 'Dulces exuviae' (Book iv. 651–4) appeared about 1500, when Margaret of Austria allowed a setting by Marbriano de Orto and an anonymous version to be included in her chanson album (Brussels, Royal Library, Ms. 228). Settings of this text have also survived by Ghiselin, Josquin,

---

[8] Trans. by Dr and Mrs H. Bodewitz, Utrecht.

[9] *Horace Satires, Epistles and 'Ars poetica'*, with an Eng. trans. by H. Rushton Fairclough (London and Cambridge, Mass., 1970), 281–3.

[10] See E. Lowinsky, 'Adrian Willaert's Chromatic "Duo" Re-examined', *Tijdschrift van de Vereniging voor Nederlandse Muziekgeschiedenis*, 18 (1956), 1–36.

Willaert, and Lasso. Willaert's version was published in 1547 by Susato in Antwerp. The rhythm of his music is completely determined by the text, and the threat of Dido's approaching death is expressed in both melody and rhythm. This composition shows that Willaert too was affected by the influence of humanism (see Ex. 37).

EX. 37

Another passage from Dido's lament (Book iv. 305–19) inspired Cypriano de Rore to write the most monumental Virgil motet of the Renaissance, *Dissimulare etiam sperasti perfide*. This is in three sections, beginning with five voices and ending with seven; the increase in scoring brings the setting to a climax, symbolizing Dido's sorrow. Rore's motet is found in one of the magnificent manuscripts which Albrecht V, the first Renaissance Prince of Bavaria, had compiled. Hans Mielich illustrated the music with large miniatures, and even the portrait of the composer was included in the manuscript (see Fig. 47).

THE NETHERLANDERS AND THE GERMAN LIED

The heading of this section is the title of an extensive study of this subject which appeared in Berlin in 1938.[11] A repertoire of more than a thousand German Lieder, some of them religious, survives from the work of over thirty composers of Netherlands origin. Here we shall deal only with Heinrich Isaac, Orlando di Lasso, and Jacob Regnart.

The German songs of Isaac belong almost entirely to the genre of the *Tenorlied*: the song is presented by a singer, while two or three instruments

---

[11] H. Osthoff, *Die Niederländer und das deutsche Lied, 1400–1640* (Berlin, 1938; 2nd edn., Tutzing, 1967).

play parts in counterpoint. The melody may be a simple folksong or a *Hofweise*. Melodies of the latter type were more artificial in nature, stemming from the tradition of the medieval Minnesang. Isaac also based a number of two-part canons on song melodies. In *Zwischen perg und tieffe tal* the bass and tenor sing the song melody, while instruments play the superius and alto. *Wohlauf, gut G'sell, von hinnen* proves that the court song and folksong could be merged together. Isaac chose this Minnelied as the basis for two of his Masses; he also wrote a Lied with the title *Comment peult avoir joye* which, interestingly enough, is based on the same melody.

EX. 38

Other compositions, by Josquin and others, show that around 1500 this melody was known in both Germany and France. The sources do not indicate the language area in which the song originated, but the relationship between words and music points to its German roots.

Isaac's best-known Lied is *Innsbruck, ich muss dich lassen*. Two different vocal settings by him are extant; Isaac owes his fame in Germany to the version with the melody in the upper voice. Following Italian models, this Lied is exclusively vocal; simple polyphony alternates with four-part homophonic passages (see Ex. 38). After the Reformation the text was changed to 'O Welt, ich muss dich lassen', and the popularity of the Lied increased further after Paul Gerhardt set a new sacred text, 'Nun ruhen alle Wälder', to it in the seventeenth century.

Orlando di Lasso's contribution to the German Lied tradition was an unusually individual one. In the dedication of his first collection, *Newe teütsche Liedlein* of 1567, the composer refers to his compositions on Latin, Italian, French, and Dutch[12] texts, and says that his German Lieder—in contrast with this other music—were intended exclusively for the court of

---

[12] The compositions on Dutch texts have been lost.

Wilhelm, the son of Albrecht V. Thanks to Lasso's experience with the Italian and French repertoires, the solo Lied with instrumental accompaniment, the type then current in Germany, gave way in his *œuvre* to the Lied for vocal ensemble. He had a predilection for amusing texts, in which the theme of love plays a rather frequent role. The drinking-song was also important, and his works in this genre tell us that the composer drank wine in preference to beer. Unfortunately Lasso usually gives only one verse, as in the Lied which follows:

> Ich weiss mir ein Meidlein hübsch und fein,
> Hüt du dich, es kann wohl falsch und freundlich sein.
> Hüt du dich, vertrau ihr nicht
> Sie nar, nar, nar, nar, narret dich.
>
> I know a beautiful, fine girl,
> Be careful, she can be both false and friendly,
> Be careful, do not trust her,
> She is making a fool of you.

The fivefold repetition of the crucial verb *narren* (to make a fool of) gives the word an amusing effect. In *Tritt auf den Rigel von der thür* Lasso brilliantly imitates the adventures of a courting man: the impatient knocking at the door and stealing into the house contrast in the music with the invitation 'zart schönes Fräulein, stand auf!' (sweet beautiful girl, stand up!).

From the stylistic point of view Lasso's German Lieder are a mixture of French and Italian elements. The composer's native language was French, but he had to learn Italian at the early age of 13, numbered Spanish musicians among his colleagues, and found his sphere of activity in Germany; consequently he had an exceptionally strong international orientation. Lasso's wittily assembled, polyglot letters to the young Prince Wilhelm give a good idea of his disposition. On 8 and 12 October 1576 he wrote the following lines about his most recent song, *Baur, baur, was trägst du im sacke*:

... Mi piace multis multum grandemente die 6 versis pauren liedlis; faciam cantum melius quod mihi possibilis fuerat ... la chanson germanica est Jam positam in musica, et va bien, quand on la porte; s'elle est bonne ie m'en raporte; elle est un peu asses longue pour la matière quelle doit servir, ie la mostrabo cras a mastro Zanj pittore, mais nous ne pouvons rien concludere sans la presentia dil nostro rarissimo patron; venes don, segnor bon ...

(I like the six strophes of peasant song very much and I will set them to music as best as ever I can...the German song has already been set—it goes well when

EX. 39

Nun bin ich ein-mal frey, nun bin ich ein-mal frey von lie-bes ban-den,

Nun bin ich ein-mal frey, nun bin ich ein-mal frey von lie-bes ban-den,

Nun bin ich ein-mal frey, nun bin ich ein-mal frey von lie-bes ban-den,

it is borne. If it is good, I will come back to it. It is a little too long for the purpose that it should serve. Tomorrow I will show it to the painter Mr Zanj, but we cannot decide anything without the presence of our highly gifted lord. Therefore come, dear Sir.)[13]

With the work of Jacob Regnart, the German Lied came more strongly under the spell of Italian music. His Lieder were published between 1576 and 1579, and their unequalled popularity is evident from the many reprints which appeared in Nuremberg and Munich over the course of thirty-five years. No less a composer than Lasso had great respect for Regnart, and mentioned the name of his countryman in one of his sacred songs. The title-page of Regnart's collection states: 'Kurzweilige teutsche Lieder | zu dreyen stimmen | nach der art der Neapolitanen oder Welschen Villanellen' (Amusing German songs for three voices in the style of the Neapolitan or Italian *villanelle*). The characteristic parallel fifths of the *villanella* also appear in Regnart; see, for example, the passage from *Nun bin ich einmal frey von liebes banden* quoted in Ex. 39. Regnart's success with this music—even Lasso had to be satisfied with less—can be explained by its simplicity. The strophic form, the simple chords, and the choices of text apparently conformed to what people wished to hear and sing. The poem with which Regnart recommended his *Kurzweilige Lieder* proves that he wished to offer something new:

> Lass dich darum nit wenden ab,
> Das ich hierinn nit brauchet hab
> Vil zierligkeit der Music.
> Wiss, das es sich durchaus nit schick,
> Mit Villanellen hoch zu prangen,
> Und wöllen dardurch preiss erlangen
> Wirdt sein vergebens und umbsunst;
> An andre ort gehört die kunst.

[13] See H. Leuchtmann, *Orlando di Lasso. Briefe* (Wiesbaden, 1977), 208 and 212.

Do not be deterred,
That I have not used herein
Much musical elegance.
Know that it is not at all suitable
To dazzle with *villanelle*.
Wishing to receive praise for them
Will be in vain and to no avail:
Art belongs elsewhere.

In other words, the composer consciously refrained from serving art. As the following opening lines of his *villanelle* suggest, the poems he chose certainly did not demand music of great quality: Ach weib, du böses kraut (Alas woman, you are good for nothing); Ich bin gen Baden zogen (I have gone to the baths); Ich hab ein lange Zeit, meidlein um dich gefreit (Girl, I have been courting you for a long time).

THE DUTCH SONG

When in 1551 Tielman Susato issued his *Ierste musyck boexken* (see Fig. 28), containing compositions by himself, Josquin Baston, Lupus Hellinck, Jeroen Vinders, and others, he wrote in the preface:

... so my special intention has been also to bring to light the noble heavenly art of music in our Netherlands mother tongue, just as in Latin, French, and the Italian language it has spread to become very well known in all lands. And in order to realize this as soon as possible, I have with great diligence brought together the best, most artful, carefully selected songs by masters of the art, composed in our mother tongue, that it was possible for me to get, out of which I (leaving out those which through indecent words may awaken mischief) have compiled three small books, of which I now issue this first one ...

Obviously Susato saw a gap in the market. But, as we have said in the introduction to this chapter, the great Netherlands composers generally showed little interest in composing Dutch songs. Only in the second half of the sixteenth century did the repertoire broaden considerably.

One of the oldest manuscripts to contain polyphonic Dutch songs dates from the end of the fourteenth century, and was possibly copied in Strasburg; it is now in Prague. But the most extensive source (London, British Library, Add. Ms. 35087) dates only from the beginning of the sixteenth century. The original owner was an official at the Dutch court in Malines. The manuscript contains twenty-five Dutch songs for three voices, and all are anonymous. *T'meiskin was ionck* is ascribed in other

Het ierſte muſyck boexken mit
VIER PARTYEN DAER INNE
Begrepen zyu xxviij nieuue amoreuſe liedekẽs in onſer neder
duytſcher talen, Gecomponeert by diuerſche com-
poniſten, zeer luſtich om ſingen en ſpelen op
alle muſicale Inſtrumẽten Ghedruckt
Tantuuerpẽ by Tielmã Suſato
vuonẽde uoer die nieuue vua-
ghe Inden Crom horn.

TENOR.

CVM GRATIA ET PRIVILEGIO.
ANNO. M. CCCCC. LI.

Ex
Biblioth.Regia
Beroline nſi.

FIG. 28. Title-page of the first edition of Dutch polyphonic songs, which appeared in Flanders in 1551. *Het ierste musyck boexken* was the first in a series of eleven such music prints published by Tielman Susato in Antwerp. Together with the second, third, and seventh *musyck boexken*, the partbook shown here has been preserved in the Biblioteka Jagiellonska in Cracow since the Second World War. (See also Fig. 4.)

sources to Isaac, Johannes Japart, and Obrecht; it also appears in Petrucci's *Odhecaton* with an additional alto part. In the original version the folksong lies in the tenor, while the upper and lower parts (for instruments or voices) move in counterpoint (see Ex. 40). There are few songs from around 1500. One considerable contribution to the repertoire, comprising twenty songs, was made by Johannes Ghiselin and Jacob Obrecht. Unfortunately the texts of all but one of these songs, which are not preserved in Netherlands sources, are missing. Only the text of

EX. 40

EX. 41

Ghiselin's *Ghy syt die werste boven al*, published by Susato, is known. Attempts to search for texts using the Dutch Folksong Archives have yielded hardly any results.

One of the chanson albums of Margaret of Austria contains the four-part *Mijn hert altijt heeft verlanghen* by Pierre de la Rue. Several anonymous arrangements of this courtly, melancholy love-song are known; to judge by the large number of sources, that by La Rue must have been much favoured. In Margaret's album all the parts are provided with text. The superius and tenor form the structural basis of the composition (see Ex. 41).

After the love-song the guild song, drinking-song, and morality song were the most popular genres in the Low Countries. Lupus Hellinck has left a nice example of the last category. Its subject is a lottery, which was in fact often an occasion for singing songs; in order to restore St James's Church in Antwerp a lottery was held in which the prizes consisted of songbooks.[14] The giving of prizes is parodied in a lively dialogue between the various pairs of voices:

> Compt alle voort bij twee bij drij
> en hoort u lot met zinne blije
> Wat u toesent fortune loterije

. . . .

[14] See Lenaerts, op. cit. (above, n. 1), 40.

Die gerne poit en is beroit
Wat zal men hem borghen segt ons thediet—
Niet!

Come forth in twos and threes
And hear your fate with a happy mind
Which the chance of the lottery is giving you.

. . . .

He who likes to drink and is impoverished
What credit shall he be given: we rightly say—
Naught!

Apart from his Dutch psalm-settings, some three- and four-part secular songs by Clemens non Papa have survived. They were issued by four publishers, in Antwerp, Louvain, and Maastricht. Although Clemens readily used imitative technique in his vocal ensemble music, quite a number of homophonic passages occur in these pieces. *Te schepe waert* is perhaps a guild song, and it has a moral in store. The men are dressing themselves for the feast:

Helpt ons de feeste vermeeren,
met vraukens fyn:
elc kies de syn,
en houts altijd in eeren!

Help us enlarge the festivities,
with fine women:
each choose his own,
and hold her always in honour!

The Dutch song tradition of the sixteenth century also includes a totally different type of text, which it owes to Cornelis Schuyt. As a university town, Leiden gave a considerable impetus to the writing of poetry in the Dutch language. In his collection *Hollandsche Madrigalen*, published in Leiden in 1603, Schuyt wished to show 'dat onse taele niet onbequaem en is om de vrolikheyt die in de Musijke verheyscht wordet, sangwijs lustig uyt te drukken' (that our language is not incapable of expressing cheerfully in song the merriness which is demanded in music). Unfortunately only three of the original set of (probably) five partbooks have been preserved. There are six wedding poems and one elegy among the sixteen texts. The poetry is not always of the highest quality, but this proves not to have had any effect on the level of Schuyt's music. Despite this the composer's 'new' music seems to have been imitated very little. Only one other collection appeared: Cornelis Padbrué's three- and four-part *Kusies, in 't Latijn gheschreven door Johannes Secundus, ende in duytsche vaersen ghesteldt door Jacob Westerbaen* (Kisses, written in Latin by Johannes Secundus, and translated into Dutch verses by Jacob Westerbaen), which was published in Haarlem in 1631.

5

Instrumental Music

THERE is a certain amount of instrumental music among the works of the fifty Netherlands musicians discussed in this book, but this repertoire can scarcely be regarded as having great historical significance. On closer inspection it emerges that only Alexander Agricola, Adrian Willaert, Jacob Buus, and Jan Pieterszoon Sweelinck made important contributions to the development of music for instrumental ensemble or keyboard instruments.

In evaluating this repertoire one must, however, realize that notated instrumental music was only just emerging as an area of artistic activity in the Renaissance. Indeed, few instrumental pieces from the Middle Ages have survived. Because the Church had so many objections to performances by minstrels, it was a long time before musicians who had been educated in an ecclesiastical atmosphere—as in the Netherlands—applied themselves to this art-form. But there is also another explanation for the fact that we encounter notated instrumental music rather late. The art of the instrumentalist was dependent on his skill in improvisation, guidelines for which were given in various ancient treatises. It was perhaps precisely because of this skill that the blind organists Francesco Landini (*d* 1397), Conrad Paumann (*d* 1473), and Antonio de Cabezón (*d* 1566) won such great fame. The story is told about Sweelinck that one evening he improvised over 'De lustelijcke Mey', 'not being able to stop, such was the very sweet humour he was in, pleasing us his friends, pleasing also himself'.[1]

Many documents prove that the instrumentalist began to win increasing recognition in the Renaissance. The Church also changed its attitude: in 1649 the chapter of St John's Church in Utrecht raised the salary of the blind carilloneur Jacob van Eyck, 'provided that he sometimes in the evenings entertains people strolling in the churchyard with the sound of his flutes'.[2]

The solo music for lute and keyboard from the sixteenth century consists mainly of transcriptions of vocal compositions such as chan-

---

[1] See F. Noske, 'John Bull's Dutch Carol', *Music and Letters*, 46 (1963), 329.

[2] See D. van den Hul, *Klokkenkunst te Utrecht tot 1700, met bijzondere aandacht voor het aandeel hierin van Jhr. Jacob van Eyck* (Stichtse Historische Reeks, viii; n.p., 1982), 146.

sons and madrigals. Sometimes the 'arrangers' are known, but mostly they remain anonymous. Only a few of them, for example Emmanuel Adriaenssen from Antwerp, made their names as composers as well. But whereas the clavichord, harpsichord, and lute were already being heard in sitting-rooms in the first half of the sixteenth century (see Fig. 29), the earliest Netherlands music written for these instruments dates from the second half of the century.

FIG. 29. This portrait by the Flemish painter Jan Van Hemessen shows that the clavichord was already played in the Netherlands in the 1530s. The lady depicted here is possibly Eleonora of Austria, the eldest sister of Charles V, though the painting was also seen as a portrait of Mary Magdalene. Worcester, Mass., Worcester Art Museum.

landum eaā luvuria
malum q̄ accusare
aliq̄to facilius est
qua vitur operi mō insernt. Non
quidem ut illis honorem rapiat
sed ut seipm̄ recognoscent ad
penitentiā impelli possit iungat

aut ab emendatione separent̄ q̄ eio
mentis errore cōnere
en ceste partie valerius commence
son vo̾ liure qui est det die z det
fait dignes de memore de la cite
de comme z det estrangiers ougl
a prēs ce que valerius est vng liure

F I G. 30. Musicians were often to be found at public baths. This illustration, by an anonymous miniaturist, appears in a copy of Valerius Maximus, *De dictis et factis Romanorum* prepared for Antoine of Burgundy about 1470. Berlin, Staatsbibliothek Preussischer Kulturbesitz, Ms. Rehd. 2.

The contribution of the Netherlanders to instrumental music must therefore be sought exclusively in the field of newly composed works. With the exception of the keyboard music of Buus and Sweelinck and a few lute pieces by the latter, the Netherlanders with whom this book is concerned wrote only for two- to six-part ensembles. Josquin and his contemporaries Agricola, Obrecht, Isaac, and Brumel provided between them a particularly enthralling repertoire, whose boundaries are however anything but clear. Since so many ensemble pieces are settings of a well-known song in which the *cantus prius factus* appears as far as possible in its original form, we generally do not know if the song melody was performed vocally or instrumentally. In other words, we do not know whether we are considering a solo song with instrumental accompaniment, or a purely instrumental piece. The texts of these songs were always in the vernacular; when they appear in manuscripts or printed editions outside their original language area, the text is usually omitted. Some of these song arrangements will be examined more closely below.

RICERCARS

Apart from song arrangements, there exist three-part pieces with short titles, some of which seem to refer to a particular person: *La Alfonsina* (Ghiselin), *La Bernardina* (Josquin), *La Martinella* (Martini and Isaac), *La Stangetta* (Weerbecke). The imitative character of this late-fifteenth-century music points forward to the three- and four-part ricercars which Adrian Willaert would publish in 1540 and 1551. The term for this form, which was originally used only in Italy, is related to the verb *ricercare* (to search, namely for the theme). Ex. 42 shows, by way of comparison, the first bars of Martini's *La Martinella* (*a*) and those of Willaert's *Recercar decimo* from the edition of 1540 (*b*). The title-page of the collection *Musica nova*, published in Venice in 1540, declares that Willaert's ricercars can be sung—as polyphonic solfeggi in this case—or played on an organ or other instruments; despite this the format of the edition lends itself more to ensemble performance than to use at the organ. *Musica nova* was in fact published in four separate partbooks. Naturally, the organist could certainly put the works into tablature, that is, make a score from the various parts. It is interesting that a ricercar by Jacob Buus has been preserved in two versions, one for ensemble (Ex. 43*a*) and one for organ (*b*). Applicants for the post of organist at St Mark's, Venice had, among other things, to be capable of improvising a ricercar; according to a Venetian document Buus understood this art particularly well.

EX. 42
(a)

(b)

EX. 43
(a)

(b)

DANCE MUSIC

The Netherlanders rose to the occasion in the field of dance music too. Ghiselin and Josquin made arrangements of 'La Spagna', one of the best-known *basse danse* melodies from the fifteenth century. A feature of the rhythmic notation of these melodies was the use of equal note-values (see Fig. 31), which were played, for example, on a sackbut or low shawm. One to three musicians with shawms improvised over this, and they had to adapt themselves to the choreography of the dance. Such groups of instruments were called an *alta*, since they used *instruments hauts* (loud-sounding instruments). The musical character of arrangements by Ghiselin and Josquin comes into its own when it is performed by such an ensemble.

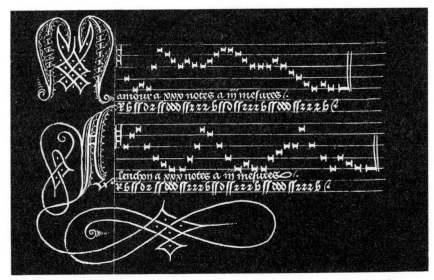

FIG. 31. Folio containing the *basses dances Mamour* and *Alenchon*, from a small music book belonging to Margaret of Austria. The black paper is written on with gold and silver ink. The letters under the melody indicate the dance steps. Brussels, Royal Library, Ms. 9085.

Cornelis Schuyt made one of the most remarkable contributions to Netherlands dance music. His set of six-part pavans and galliards, published in Leiden in 1611, comprises twelve pairs of dances, the first of each in duple time and the second in triple time. At the beginning and end of his collection the composer placed instrumental canzonas, of which the first bears the title *Fortuna guida* and the second *La Barca*. These words contain a wish for victory, and at the same time form a pun on his name: 'May Fortune steer the ship [*schuyt*]'. The regularity of the metrical structure suggests that this music was probably intended at the time to accompany dancing.

Sixty years before the Leiden publication, *Het derde musyck boexken* appeared in Antwerp, containing dance music composed and published by Tielman Susato. Susato based these fifty-seven dances on popular tunes of the time; most of them therefore have subtitles such as *Mille regretz*, *La bataille*, and *Den hoboecken dans*. The collection is the oldest known printed source of ensemble dance music from the Low Countries (see also Fig. 28).

SONG ARRANGEMENTS

'Tandernaken op den Rijn' (which refers to the German town of Andernach) was a favourite song in the Low Countries; it was sung for more than a century. While the earliest instrumental arrangement of it (that by Tyling in Trent 87) comes from the first half of the fifteenth century, the text still appears in the *Antwerps Liedboek* of 1544, in which it is called 'Een oudt liedeken' (An old song). The song deals with two

EX. 44

young girls who confide in one another about their amorous affairs. There are three-part arrangements by Alexander Agricola, Antoine Brumel, and Jacob Obrecht, each of whom places the melody in the middle part. Brumel and Obrecht quote it in an almost unornamented form, whereas Agricola treats it with such rich coloratura that it is scarcely recognizable. The arrangements resemble each other in their imitative outer parts, and their playful style makes them enjoyable to perform. It is therefore no wonder that the pieces by Agricola and Obrecht, which were first published by Petrucci in Venice at the beginning of the sixteenth century, were still being arranged for lute in Germany thirty years later.

A song even more frequently arranged by Netherlanders was the three-part *De tous biens plaine* by Hayne van Ghizeghem. The text is a poetic ode to Woman. The splendidly balanced melody of the superius makes it easy to see why Hayne's rondeau was one of the most widely disseminated songs of the fifteenth century: about twenty-five sources of it are known. The arrangements which deserve pride of place are those by Tinctoris, Ghiselin, Josquin, and Agricola, on account of their lively character. Josquin changes Hayne's bass into a two-part canon at the unison in which the second part is separated from the first by only one beat; this is humorously expressed in the text for the lowest part, 'Petrus et Johannes currunt [run] in puncto'. Josquin gives the instrumentalists a difficult task here (see Ex. 44).

In the works of Agricola, who arranged *De tous biens plaine* five times,

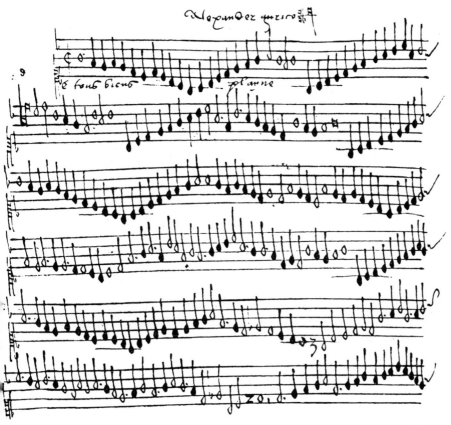

FIG. 32. The beginning of the superius part of *De tous biens plaine*, one of the five instrumental arrangements which Alexander Agricola made of this song. Segovia, Cancionero de la Catedral.

instrumental virtuosity is still greater. In each case Hayne's tenor melody forms the backbone of the composition. The newly composed parts contain long scale motifs, short sequences, punctuated rhythms, syncopations, and triplet rhythms of varying types (see Fig. 32). Perhaps these pieces were intended for a viol ensemble; the range of the parts would suggest this. The Renaissance viol had already appeared in Aragon in the 1470s, having probably been introduced in Italy by way of the Aragonese court in Naples, where Agricola received a princely reception as an instrumentalist. Tinctoris's arrangement, a duo, is also shown to full advantage when played on viols. While the counterpoint in four of Agricola's arrangements is distinguished by a great deal of variety, that of

E X. 45

8 De tous biens plaine

E X. 46

the fifth is more like a study for two lutes. The upper and lower parts
consist entirely of quickly moving crotchets (see Ex. 45); the use of a
plectrum lends the piece a brilliant character.

FORTUNA

In the previous chapter we have seen that the goddess Fortuna inspired
the Netherlanders to numerous vocal song-settings; she also left her traces
in the field of instrumental music. Some composers, remarkably, gave
musical form to one of her best-known attributes, the turning wheel. A
piece by Isaac with the title *Corri Fortuna* has survived in which, towards
the end, the four parts sequentially imitate the circular movement of the
wheel (see Ex. 46). In this piece Isaac recalls the vocal setting by Martini in
which the bass revolves in a *circulatio* figure (see p. 90).

Another Fortuna composition raises absorbing questions for the music
historian: Josquin's *Fortuna dun gran tempo*,[3] a piece for three instruments
based on an Italian folksong which was also used by Isaac in his quodlibet
Donna di dentro. The most characteristic element is the opening of the

[3] See E. Lowinsky, 'The Goddess Fortuna in Music with a Special Study of Josquin's "Fortuna
dun gran tempo"', *The Musical Quarterly*, 29 (1943), 45–77, and J. van Benthem, 'Fortuna in Focus.
Concerning "Conflicting" Progressions in Josquin's "Fortuna dun gran tempo"', *Tijdschrift van de
Vereniging voor Nederlandse Muziekgeschiedenis*, 30 (1980), 1–50.

melody, a falling series of five notes; it is this motif that Josquin exploits. The superius opens the composition with the motif on g^1 without a flat in the key signature; the tenor enters with the same motif on c^1 and has one flat in the key signature; the third part, the contratenor, enters with the same motif on f and has two flats in the key signature. In the course of the piece the differences in key signature give rise to some harmonic progressions which are striking to present-day ears, but which in the fifteenth century were not unusual in the context of the Lydian mode.

EX. 47

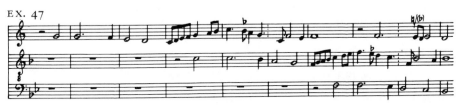

Following an ancient tradition, as late as 1482 the Spanish music theorist Ramos de Pareia related the structure of the modes to the cosmos by ascribing each mode to a particular planet, while each planet was in turn linked to a particular temperament. Josquin's *Fortuna dun gran tempo* is in the Lydian and Hypolydian modes, which Ramos associated respectively with Fortuna and Venus, the goddesses of fortune and love. In the Renaissance they were often regarded as rivals, as witnessed in the text of *Fortuna desperata* (see p. 90). The combination of the two modes in Josquin's *Fortuna dun gran tempo*, in which the original text also alludes to Love's happiness being threatened by Fortuna, is thus a splendid specimen of the way in which this composer used musical means to a symbolic end (see Ex. 47).

JAN PIETERSZOON SWEELINCK

The theme of Fortuna in Netherlands instrumental music is closely connected with humanism in Italian Renaissance culture. It seems to be a world away from the city of Amsterdam, ruled by a Calvinist council, where Jan Pieterszoon Sweelinck was active as city organist at the Oude Kerk. Sweelinck's keyboard music, the high point of a repertoire to which Henderick Speuy in Dordrecht and Pieter Cornet in Brussels also contributed, nevertheless includes variations on a Fortuna song. Sweelinck took as his starting-point the English song 'Fortune my foe', which appeared in many Netherlands song collections from 1603 onwards. Valerius set the poem 'Stort tranen uyt' (Shed tears) to this melody in his *Nederlandsche Gedenck-clank* (see Ex. 48). The composition consists of three variations, including a setting of the melody; it was customary to count the melody itself among the variations in this period. The variations on 'Est-ce Mars' and 'Mein junges Leben hat ein End'' are conceived on a larger scale and require a more virtuoso technique. The scale figures and arpeggiated chords alternating between left and right hands, the imitations and sequence motifs, repeated notes and parallel thirds all make great demands on the performer. Sweelinck's variation technique is perhaps based on the Spanish tradition of the mid-sixteenth century (Cabezón), which came to the Netherlands through England. Lute collections such as *Florida* by Joachim van den Hove, published in

EX. 48

Stem: Engelsche Fortuyn.

Tort tranéuyt, schreyt luyde! weét en treurt! O dag! o dag!
Och't dunct my dat myn herte barst en scheurt !

o doncker droeve

dag !   Wat isser al   gehuyl en groot geklag !

Utrecht in 1601, and the Thysius manuscript[4] show that composers were internationally minded even in the Northern Netherlands, just like their predecessors from Flanders, Brabant, and Hainault. These manuscripts contain a varied collection of arrangements of foreign monophonic and polyphonic songs. Sweelinck quite frequently chose melodies of German origin for his organ chorales, and also for his sets of variations. Perhaps the fact that he had German pupils was a contributory factor in this.

In his toccatas he sometimes used the same principles of composition as organists of St Mark's in Venice: a homophonic introduction is followed by a fugato, and the piece closes with expansive passage-work. Though these compositions have been conceived as free improvisations, the various sections add up to a marvellously balanced construction.

Our final category comprises Sweelinck's fantasias and ricercars. These compositions link Sweelinck, as a member of the Netherlands School, to a tradition that goes back by way of Buus to Willaert. His contrapuntal technique is masterly. The main theme of a work functions as a cell which may undergo all types of rhythmic transformations in the course of the

---

[4] Now in the University Library, Leiden.

Fig. 33. Trumpeters and drummers at the funeral procession in the solemnities for the death of Charles V in 1558. This engraving by Jan and Lucas Duetecum, after a drawing by Jeroen Wellens de Cock, was printed by Plantin in Antwerp in 1559. Brussels, Royal Library.

piece while remaining recognizable; subsidiary themes provide melodic variety. The shortest fantasia lasts forty-four bars: it is a bicinium beginning with an extended canon, after which comes an imitative section built from charming short motifs. The longest fantasia forms a sharp contrast with this one: in the course of 317 bars of music this piece unfolds a panorama of contrapuntal subtleties in which the principle of *varietas* sets the tone. Sweelinck's echo fantasias earn him a special place in the history of keyboard music. Echos were very much liked in this period: they were used first in vocal music, for example by Lasso in his *O là, o che bon eccho*. One can also find them in Dutch literature: Vondel uses the echo effect between the stranger and the resonance of the church in his poem 'Gesprek op het graf ' on the death in 1619 of Johan van Oldenbarnevelt:

Stranger: Wat zal men Barnevelt, die 't juk zocht af te keren?
Echo: Eren
Stranger: Wat wordt de Dwingeland, die 't Recht te machtig was?
Echo: As
Stranger: What will Barnevelt receive, who sought to cast off the yoke?
Echo: Honour.
Stranger: What will become of the Tyrant, who was too strong for justice?
Echo: Ash.[5]

Sweelinck's echo fantasias are written for a two-manual organ. The counterpoint, which is not based on a fixed theme in these pieces,

[5] *De Werken van Vondel*, ii (Amsterdam, 1929), 754.

EX. 49

EX. 50

alternates with homophonic passages in which the various types of echo effect are exploited by changing manuals or octave transposition (see Ex. 49).

The most famous of the fantasias is perhaps the so-called chromatic one. Here the main theme is composed of a chromatically descending series of six notes; there are also two diatonic subsidiary themes, which accompany the main theme and neutralize the severity of the chromaticism. Ex. 50 shows the main theme and the first subsidiary one. The rhythmic movement becomes gradually faster, but towards the end of the composition it enters a more peaceful vein. In this work, more clearly than in any other, Sweelinck demonstrates his importance as the final representative of the renowned Netherlands tradition. The experimental chromatic ideas that were introduced by Willaert, Rore, and the young Lasso in the mid-sixteenth century are realized here within a stable structure.

6

The Position of the Composer in Society

I N so far as the surviving documents allow one to form an impression of the position of the Netherlands musician in society in the fifteenth and sixteenth centuries, it seems reasonable to conclude that, with some exceptions, little distinguishes it from the position of musicians in our own time. To progress from this general statement, it is worth realizing that the composer held a particular place among musicians. The composer had more chance to be remembered than the man who went from village to village with his hurdy-gurdy. And it is understandable that documents from the past have the most to say about the most talented people.

A sketch of the composer's significance for Renaissance society must take as its point of departure the place which this society assigned to *ars musicae*, music. From the time when the concept of *artes liberales* was introduced, music was one of these seven liberal arts, namely, one of the seven areas of knowledge worthy of a free-born man, the opposite of the manual work of the slave. In the Middle Ages the concept of the *septem artes* determined the programme of studies at the universities. The first set of three, called the trivium, consisted of grammar, logic, and rhetoric, and the other four, the quadrivium, comprised arithmetic, geometry, astronomy, and music.

Though *ars musica* primarily meant the science of music, the practitioner of polyphonic, or indeed 'learned', music generally enjoyed great respect. Composers were spared the social prejudice that painters and sculptors, for example, still met even in the Renaissance because their work was regarded as manual and because they frequently had little education. In contrast to his artistic colleague, whose art did not belong to the *artes liberales* and who was unable to work without dirtying his hands, the composer contributed to an élite, almost scientific work.

Naturally not every choirboy was musically creative. But in principle a boy with a beautiful voice had the prospect of good opportunities. Admission to a choir school, a type of institution which flourished in the bishoprics of the Low Countries, could lead to a brilliant career, and this was especially true when musical aptitude went hand in hand with intelligence. Many a celebrated composer was discovered in his youth.

GUILLAUME DUFAY

In the accounts of the Cathedral of Cambrai a certain 'Willemet puer altaris' appears in 1409/10, in 1410/11 a 'Willermus', and in 1413/14 one 'Willermus du Fayt clericus altaris'. Early in the 1420s Guillaume Dufay, the person mentioned here, composed some works which show that he was then in the service of the Malatesta in Pesaro and Rimini. His move from the Netherlands to Italy may have been arranged in the town of Constance, where a council was held in the years 1414–18. The Bishop of Cambrai, Pierre d'Ailly, and Carlo Malatesta both played an important role in this council. After a creative life of almost half a century during which the composer maintained contacts with ecclesiastical and secular dignitaries, with artists and scholars, he died on 27 November 1474.

Dufay's gravestone (see Fig. 34) was rediscovered by chance in 1859: it seems to have remained upside-down for a long time, covering the cesspit of a canon's house in Cambrai. The four corners of the stone (which measures 80 × 90 cm.) are decorated with the composer's musical monogram. The inscription indicates that he had taken a degree in canon law, but Dufay counts as a man of letters in another way too. His will—the report of the executor runs to no less than sixty-five pages—contains a list of books which includes writings of classical antiquity. The mastery with which Dufay used classical metres in some of his Latin poems proves his thorough literary training. He was certainly familiar with the principles of rhetoric. As a canon of the cathedral in Cambrai Dufay enjoyed great respect. In 1461 he led a group of woodcutters and inspected the dikes of the canal; in 1462 he managed the *Office du four et du vin*, and in this capacity he perhaps provided his great colleague Ockeghem with bread and wine during his stay in Cambrai.[1] Neither did the composer do badly from the financial point of view, since he held several prebends. On his visit to Ferrara in 1437 he received twenty golden ducats from Niccolò d'Este, whose son Leonello paid the same amount into Dufay's account at the Borromei bank in Bruges six years later. On his death the composer left a fortune of almost 2,000 Parisian livres. An inventory of the possessions of the cathedral in Cambrai compiled by Dufay shows that he was the donor of a precious gilded silver reliquary.

---

[1] See C. Wright, 'Dufay at Cambrai: Discoveries and Revisions', *Journal of the American Musicological Society*, 28 (1975), 208.

FIG. 34. Guillaume Dufay's gravestone. In the left foreground Dufay is seen waiting for the resurrection of the dead; behind him stands St Waudru with her two children. The inscription announces that the composer was, among other things, a graduate in canon law and choirboy and later canon at the cathedral in Cambrai. The stone lay in the church until it was demolished in 1796. Lille, Musée des Beaux-Arts.

Loyset Compère wrote his so-called 'singers' prayer' before the composer's death. In the second half of this composition which is dedicated to Mary, blessing is implored for a number of named singers. Dufay stands at the top of the list, and is called 'luna totius musice atque cantorum lumine' (moon of all music, light of singers). Perhaps the composer was also commemorated in elegies after his death,[2] but none has survived.

---

2 See D. Fallows, *Dufay* (London, 1982), 83.

FIG. 35. Inlay work in wood by Antonio and Paolo Mola, of the studio of Isabella d'Este (early sixteenth century), showing the clefless puzzle canon *Prenez sur moi votre exemple* by Johannes Ockeghem. The name of the composer appears in the centre above the stave. Mantua, Palazzo ducale.

JOHANNES OCKEGHEM

In this respect the situation of Johannes Ockeghem was completely different. He is recalled in four poems, two of which were set to music. Some quotations give an impression of these laments. The longest is by Guillaume Cretin: the poet laments the musician in 420 lines. In his dream he receives the news of Ockeghem's death:

> Il est donc mort? c'est mon; mais qui? helas.
> C'est Okergan le vaillant Tresorier
> De Sainct Martin, qui eust grant tresor hier.

Is he dead then? it's true; but who? alas!
It's Ockeghem, the worthy treasurer[3]
Of St Martin's, who had great treasure here.

The muses sing his praise:

> Que on l'appelloit la perle de musique,
> Who was called the pearl of music,

and the kings he so faithfully served:

> Par quarante ans et plus il a servy,
> Sans quelque ennuy en sa charge et office
> De troys roys a tant l'amour desservy.
>
> He served for forty years and more
> Without any trouble in his duties and position,
> Under three kings he earned so much affection.

Cretin also addressed himself to Ockeghem's colleagues:

> Agricolla, Verbonnet, Prioris,
> Josquin Desprez, Gaspar, Brunel, Compere,
> Ne parlez plus de joyeux chantz ne ris,
> Mais composez ung Ne recorderis,
> Pour lamenter nostre maistre et bon pere.
>
> Agricola, Verbonnet, Prioris,
> Josquin des Prez, Gaspar, Brumel, Compère,
> Speak no more of happy songs or laugh,
> But compose a lament,
> To mourn our master and good father.

Josquin set the elegy by Jean Molinet to music, while that to a text by
Erasmus was composed by Johannes Lupi. It is certainly due to Josquin's
setting that the 'Déploration' by Molinet is so well known. Inspired by
Cretin's poem (line 277: 'Sus Molinet, dormez vous, ou resvez?'), Molinet
wrote a touching lament which closes with the lines:

> Acoutrez vous d'habits de deuil,
> Josquin, Piersson, Brumel, Compere,
> Et plourez grosses larmes d'oeil:
> Perdu avez vostre bon pere.

---

[3] See p. 169.

> Put on the garments of mourning,
> Josquin, La Rue, Brumel, Compère,
> And weep great tears, from your eyes,
> You have lost your good father.

Some have found it surprising that Erasmus could also be numbered among the mourners. There is in fact some doubt whether the great humanist sincerely appreciated the polyphonic music of the Netherlanders: he expressed himself critically on this subject more than once. Possibly Erasmus wrote the text at the request of the Bishop of Cambrai, whose service he entered as secretary in 1493. His Latin poem begins as follows:

> Ergone conticuit
> Vox illa nobilis,
> Aurea vox Okegi?
>
> Has it been silenced for ever
> Such a noble voice,
> The golden voice of Ockeghem?

It has been suggested that by using the words 'golden voice', Erasmus wished to allude to the great riches that Ockeghem owed to his musical ability. As treasurer (without the obligation of residence) at the Abbey of St Martin in Tours he enjoyed a huge income. His main function, which he fulfilled for thirty years, was that of *maître de chapelle* at the French court. Yet it is worth remembering that Ockeghem held a position which included more than singing and composing. The large reimbursement of 275 livres which Ockeghem received in 1470 in connection with expenses during a diplomatic mission to Spain proves that he was a confidant of the French king. In the 'Chant royal' of 1523 by Nicolle Le Vestu, dedicated to Ockeghem, the composer was described as follows:

> Okghem, très docte en art mathématique,
> Aritméticque, aussy geométrie,
> Astrologie et mesmement musique . . .
>
> Ockeghem, so skilled in mathematics,
> Arithmetic and geometry,
> Astrology and even music . . .

Here it is strikingly clear how thoroughly the practice of composition was founded on the basis of a broad education, and how close the *ars musicae* still was to the other arts of the quadrivium in this period. Apart from Ockeghem, several other Netherlands composers of the fifteenth century conceived mathematical structures for their compositions (see pp. 32, 59, and 78 ff.).

JOSQUIN DES PREZ

The details sketched above of the status enjoyed by Dufay and Ockeghem may also be applied, *mutatis mutandis*, to later masters such as Adrian Willaert, Cypriano de Rore, Orlando di Lasso, and Philippus de Monte. The renown which Josquin des Prez still attracted for decades after his death in 1521 is a measure of that which he enjoyed during his long life. The place which he occupied in musical life was unequalled by any other composer. The Florentine Cosimo Bartoli wrote as follows in 1567:

It is known that Ockeghem was, as it were, the first in his day to rediscover music when it was almost extinguished, just as Donatello in his time breathed new life into sculpture. It can be said of Josquin, Ockeghem's pupil, that in music he was a natural prodigy, just as our own Michelangelo Buonarotti has been in architecture, painting, and sculpture. For just as no one until now has rivalled Josquin as a composer, so Michelangelo still stands lonely at the summit of all those who have practised his arts. Both have opened the eyes of all those who rejoice in these arts or who will rejoice in the future.[4]

Even if eulogies such as this are relative, it is indeed impressive that even in Italy Josquin's name caused such admiration in the middle of the sixteenth century. Not for nothing was his music used time and again as a model. And the number of pieces suspected to be falsely ascribed to him amounts to at least a third of the size of his actual *œuvre*. As late as 1554 a piece in homage of Josquin by Jacquet de Mantua appeared in Venice: in this composition, *Dum vastos Adriae fluctus*, not only are the opening words of well-known works by Josquin quoted (in the manner of le Vestu's poem about Ockeghem), but the composer also introduces musical quotations. In the light of Josquin's posthumous reputation it is surprising that only twenty-three archival references have been found relating to his biography. It is no exaggeration to say that there is no other composer of Josquin's importance in the history of Western music about whom so little is known.

---

[4] Cosimo Bartoli, *Ragionamenti accademici ... sopra alcuni luoghi difficili di Dante* (Venice, 1567), fo. 35v.

Orland von Laſſen Muſicus in Bayeren.

Rlandus iſt zu Berga im Hennigauw deß 1568, 1530 jar erboren. Wie er ſiben jar alt worde/ rathe man jn zu der ſchul/damit er in der geſchufft vnderwiſen wurde: als er dieſe ergriffen/hat er ſich im 1539 jar mit allem ernſt auff die Muſica vnd das geſang begeben/vnd iſt durch ſein hälle lieblicheſtim menglichẽ angenem geweſen. Wie er dieſe Luſt erlernet vn vnder dẽ Knabẽ gern geſungen/hat man jn zu dem dritten malen heimlich auß der ſchul geſtolen. Er iſt durch der elteren fleiß zu dẽ anderẽ malen wider heim gebracht worden. Zu dem dritten mal kam er nit wider/ſonder bewilliget bey Ferdinando Gonzaga dẽ Königlichen ſtatthalter in Sicilia zu verharrẽ/welcher damals vor S. Deſidier vber dẽ Keiſeriſchẽ hauffen Oberſter geweſen. Wie der Frantzöſiſche krieg ein end genommen/zoge er mit jm hinweg/vn wonet zum theil in Sicilia/zum theil in Meyland gern bey jm/biß er nach ſechs jaren angefangẽ ſein ſtim zu mutieren vnnd enderen. Alſo warde er ſeines alters im 18 jar von Conſtantino Caſtrioto gehn Neaplaß gefüret/da er dañ bey Marggraff de Laterza drey jar verharret. Nach dieſem kame er gehn Rom vnd was deß Erabiſchoff zu Florentz gaſt in die ſechs monat läg/biß er in der namhaffte Lateraniſchen kirchen S. Johannis vber die gantze Muſicam eur

P ij Oberſter

FIG. 36. The first part of Samuel Quickelberg's biography of Orlando di Lasso, translated from Latin into German. In *Teutscher Nation Heldenbuch* (Basle, 1578), 507.

ORLANDO DI LASSO

It generally follows that the later a musician was active in the Renaissance period, the more details are known about his status. This is certainly true for Orlando di Lasso. The oldest surviving portrait of this composer was painted by Hans Mielich, probably about 1560. Mielich was active as a miniaturist at the sumptuous court of Albrecht V of Bavaria. The portrait is included at the end of each of the four partbooks of the *Prophetiae Sibyllarum*; the oval inscription contains the text 'Orlandus de Lasso Aetatis suae XXVIII' (Orlando di Lasso at 28 years of age). Perhaps the most notable thing about this portrait—which is almost identical to Raphael's depiction of Castiglione—is the fact that Lasso appears more as a courtier than as a composer: the well-groomed appearance, the rich clothes, the golden ring are all features not found in earlier portraits of composers.[5]

When Mielich painted Lasso's portrait the composer was already enjoying international fame. In 1560 he received an honorary pension of 1,200 livres from Charles IX, King of France, a large sum when we consider that it was the same as that received by the court poet, Pierre de Ronsard. Likewise, from 1570 he received a pension of 150 guilders from Emperor Maximilian II. Shortly before his death in 1579 Albrecht V guaranteed his Kapellmeister a lifelong salary of 400 guilders each year. Nor did the composer lack displays of homage: the Emperor Maximilian elevated Lasso to the nobility in 1570, and in 1573 he gave him a golden chain of eighty-six ducats in weight; in 1574 Gregory XIII named him a Knight of the Golden Spur.

Though Lasso is not regarded as the greatest composer of the Netherlands School, none of his predecessors achieved a similar status. While he did not have the privilege of a university education, or the support of either his forbears or family wealth, he was none the less honoured by the powerful on account of his musical gifts. As a child of his time he rose from the ranks to be a Renaissance artist in the true sense of the term. On death he was moreover a wealthy man. He left his family two houses and various pieces of ground, and as a Christian he established two foundations 'zu seinen und seiner Erben und Nachkommen immerwährendem Gedächtnis, Trost und Heyl der Seele' (for his heirs and offspring in everlasting memory, consolation, and salvation of the soul).[6]

It is clear that not all composers of the Low Countries could boast such a reputation. The most renowned textbooks are frequently forced to describe a musician simply as, for instance, a 'Netherlands composer of the first half of the sixteenth century'. Countless musicians are known only because their compositions have been preserved by chance in a manuscript or printed edition. And even more often it is to none other than the master 'Anonymous' that music historians ascribe hundreds of compositions. In this case the composer may best be compared to a painter who is only known as 'the Master of Delft'. Such musicians, working in the service of a prince or the Church, had to be content with a simple existence. They

[5] See H. Leuchtmann, 'Orlando di Lasso oder die beseelte Verrücktheit. Zeit und Unzeit einer humanistischen Musik', *Orlando di Lasso. Musik der Renaissance am Münchener Fürstenhof*. Catalogue of exhibition in Munich, 1982 (Wiesbaden, 1982), 12.

[6] See Leuchtmann, *Orlando di Lasso. Sein Leben* (Wiesbaden, 1976), 58.

were dependent on the whim of their employer; they had many duties, but only limited rights. It must be said, however, that there were favourable exceptions. The Church particularly made some social provision, and there also were pension schemes for musicians in those days. Where musicians were dependent mainly on the town authorities, their guilds grew up quickly. There is no doubt that these organizations, which had the character of a present-day union, brought about great improvements in the social position of the musician.

Frequently wages consisted of more than money. Free board and lodging, as well as payment in kind, also played a normal part in the life of the composer. When Ockeghem presented Charles VII with a music book on the occasion of the New Year in 1454, he was rewarded by the king with four yards of scarlet. Obrecht received a similar reward from Emperor Maximilian I in 1503 for his *Missa Regina caeli*:[7] on this occasion it was fourteen yards of damask.

Naturally it is generally impossible to reach conclusions from such details regarding the composer's standard of living. Even in cases where the reward was paid in actual money it is difficult to define the amounts mentioned, given the great variations in European currency of that period.

Another function of the composer, which has not been mentioned yet, was that of music teaching. In Naples Beatrice of Aragon was directed in her studies by Johannes Tinctoris, and it is known that Heinrich Isaac gave lessons to the sons of Lorenzo de' Medici. Johannes Martini was possibly the music teacher of Isabella d'Este in Ferrara, and in Prague Philippus de Monte counted the English poetess Elizabeth Weston among his pupils. *Parthenicon*, published in Prague in 1606, was the work of this remarkable lady, who exemplified the type of woman described by Thomas More and Erasmus;[8] in it she honours her teacher in a panegyric. As far as the communication of knowledge was concerned, vocational education was of more significance for the practice of music. When Hubert Waelrant founded a music school in Antwerp in 1547, he participated in a tradition which possibly went back to the earliest years of the Netherlands School. Ockeghem, Josquin, Willaert, and Sweelinck made their names as teachers of great composers, and the influence which their compositions exerted determined to a large extent the way in which music developed.

---

[7] This Mass has been lost.

[8] See D. Busch, *English Literature in the Earlier Seventeenth Century, 1600–1660* (2nd edn., Oxford, 1948), 21 and 606.

APPENDIX

The following is an alphabetical list of fifty Netherlands composers, one or more of whose works are mentioned in this book. These composers have in some cases been chosen for the merit of one of their works rather than their general importance.

Where there is more than one way of writing the name, the other spellings are given after the most usual one. The biographical sketches and descriptions of works naturally make no claim to completeness. More detailed information can be found in the appropriate articles in *The New Grove Dictionary of Music and Musicians* (London, 1980), *Die Musik in Geschichte und Gegenwart* (Kassel, 1949–79), and monographs mentioned in these. Both reference works can be found in the music departments of university and conservatory libraries, and in some large public libraries.

AGRICOLA, Alexander (*b* 1446; *d* Valladolid, 1506)

is called a 'Belgian' in his epitaph; in sixteenth-century humanistic Latin this means 'Netherlander'. From 1471 he was in Milan in the service of Galeazzo Maria Sforza, who gave him a letter of recommendation to Lorenzo de' Medici in Florence in 1474. In 1476 he appears as 'petit vicaire' (singer of the canonic hours) in Cambrai. Afterwards he worked for some time at the French court, where he was a colleague of Ockeghem. In 1491 he is recorded as a singer in the cathedral in Florence, and in the following year he appears in Naples at the Aragonese court of Ferrante I, who sent the composer back to France at the request of Charles VIII. From 1500 he was in the court chapel of Philip the Fair, with whom he travelled to Spain for the second time in 1506; he and the king both died there during an outbreak of plague. After his death Agricola was called 'clarus vocum manuumque'; this shows that he was famous as both a singer and instrumentalist. He is also mentioned as a lute virtuoso.

Eight Masses and some Mass movements by Agricola are known. He composed Masses on *cantus prius facti* taken from chansons by Dufay, Busnois, and Ockeghem. One of his own songs, *In myne zin*, also served as the basis for a Mass. Besides his other liturgical compositions (two hymns, two Lamentations settings, and three Magnificat settings), he

The Low Countries, showing centres of music and places of birth and death of composers

wrote thirteen motets. Moreover, about fifty compositions on texts in French, Italian (three), and Dutch (two) have survived. Among his twenty-five instrumental pieces are several three- and four-part versions of Hayne van Ghizeghem's *De tous biens plaine* and Ockeghem's *D'ung aultre amer*.

BAULDEWEYN [Baldwyn], Noel (*b* c.1480; *d* Antwerp, 1530)   23
151

was *magister cantorum* at St Rombold's Church in Malines in 1509, and between 1512 and 1517 he carried out the same role at the Church of Our Lady in Antwerp.

Bauldeweyn's surviving music consists almost completely of sacred works. Seven Masses are attributed to him, though of these the *Missa Da pacem* is also found under Josquin's name. His eight motets include a *Salve regina* in which he cites the chanson *Je n'ay dueil* by Ockeghem.

BERCHEM, Jacquet de (*b* ?Berchem near Antwerp, c.1505; *d* c.1565)   93
167

was possibly a protégé of Willaert in Venice, where much of his music appeared. He is frequently confused with the French composer Jacquet de Mantua, who in 1550 published Vespers psalms in collaboration with Willaert and other composers. Some compositions cannot be ascribed to one or other of these two composers with any certainty. Together with Willaert and some Italian composers, Jacquet played an important role in the development of the madrigal. His contemporary Rabelais counted him among the most highly acclaimed musicians.

Jacquet's church music includes two Masses (one of which is based on Gombert's chanson *Mort et fortune*) and eight motets. His secular music comprises one ceremonial motet, fourteen chansons, and over 190 madrigals, the texts of which include, among others, twenty-one poems from Petrarch's *Canzoniere* and ninety-one strophes from Ariosto's *Orlando furioso*.

BINCHOIS, Gilles (de Bins dit) (*b* ?Mons, Hainault, c.1400;   5
d Soignies, 1460)   35
44
can be seen as the most important representative of the true Burgundian   96
tradition. At the age of nineteen he became organist at St Waudru's   149
Church in Mons. A few years later he was a soldier in the service of   169
the Earl of Suffolk, who was a member of the English forces in France   170
during the Hundred Years War. Binchois was already a member of

LEAL SOVVENIR

FIG. 37. According to the art historian Erwin Panofsky, Gilles Binchois was the model for this 'portrait' of the poet-musician Timothy of Miletus, painted by Jan van Eyck in 1432. If this hypothesis is correct, Binchois is the earliest composer in Western music of whom a large portrait has been preserved. London, National Gallery.

the Burgundian court chapel before 1430. In 1449 he met Dufay in Mons, and it is possible that the two composers already knew each other then. The composer held prebends from various churches (including St Donatian in Bruges), and during his last years also received a pension from the Burgundian court.

Binchois is nowadays known mainly as the composer of almost sixty French chansons, but no small number of liturgical works by him have also survived: twenty-eight Mass sections, one psalm and six Magnificats, ten antiphons, seven hymns, and some motets. His chansons (on poems by Charles d'Orléans, Alain Chartier, and Christine de Pisan among others) are mainly rooted in the tradition of the courtly song. *Comme femme desconfortée* became well known because Isaac used the chanson melody in his Mass of the same name, Josquin and Ghiselin based motets on it, and Agricola made instrumental versions of it. Many other composers in the fifteenth century chose music by Binchois as the starting-point for their own works.

BRUMEL, Antoine (*b c*.1460; *d c*.1515)

23
40
115
120
131
152

was summoned along with six other Netherlands musicians in Guillaume Cretin's lament on the death of Ockeghem to compose a *Ne recorderis*, 'pour lamenter nostre maistre et bon pere' (see p. 131). At about the age of 23 he gained the position of singer in Chartres, and three years later he appears in Geneva, where he remained until 1492. In 1497 he was a canon at the cathedral in Laon, and in the following year he was entrusted with teaching the choirboys at Notre Dame in Paris. He was associated as a singer with the court of Savoy in Chambéry for over a year from June 1501. His last known residence was the d'Este court in Ferrara (1506–10).

The works of Brumel comprise mainly church music. Mass compositions hold an important place, with fifteen complete cycles and four Credo settings. Besides a *Requiem* and the twelve-part *Missa Et ecce terrae motus*, which was still being performed under Lasso in Munich more than fifty years after the composer's death, he wrote a Mass on the hexachord ut–re–mi–fa–sol–la. As well as basing works on music by Josquin, Agricola, and himself, he also employed chant frequently. In his thirty-odd motets, liturgical texts such as antiphons, sequences, and Magnificats are the most strongly represented. His *Lamentatio Jeremiae* can also be counted in this latter category. Brumel's secular music consists of five chansons, including the notable *De tout plongiet*, and nine instrumental pieces.

BUSNOIS [de Busne], Antoine (*b c.*1430; *d* Bruges, 1492)

possibly came from a family with origins in Picardy. Before he entered the service of Charles the Bold as a singer at the court in Dijon in 1467, he was probably resident in Paris: some of his chansons, for which he certainly wrote his own texts, honour the Parisian lady Jacqueline d'Hacqueville. Moreover, a document of 1465 is known in which one 'Antonius Busnoys' is named as a singer at the Abbey of St Martin in Tours, where he was ordained. Busnois was therefore a colleague of Ockeghem in Tours. After the death of Charles in 1477, Busnois retained his position at court under Charles's daughter Mary for another five years. An archival text names him as 'prêtre chaplain' at that time. It is not known when he was finally appointed rector of the choir school of St Saviour's Church in Bruges. Busnois was one of the leading composers of his time, and his name appears in various literary and musical texts; together with Ockeghem, he is mentioned in the dedication of Tinctoris's treatise on church modes of 1476.

The works of Busnois show him as a master of the chanson; about sixty rondeaux and bergerettes have survived. In some of these, following former practice, two texts are sung at the same time. The opening words of the bergerette *Ja que lui ne* and the rondeau *Ha que ville* can be read as the name of his benefactress (see p. 99). His chanson *Bel Acueil* fittingly opens the magnificent chanson album which Tinctoris compiled for Beatrice of Aragon in the 1470s by alluding to Fair Welcome, an allegorical figure from the thirteenth-century *Roman de la Rose*, and at the same time indicating the recipient's name by means of the initial letters of the chanson's title, B and A. His known church music comprises two Masses (one on 'L'homme armé') and some hymns and antiphons. One of his motets, *Anthoni usque limina*, was written in honour of his patron saint; *In hydraulis* originated as a tribute to Ockeghem.

BUUS, Jakob (*b* ?Ghent, *c.*1500; *d* Vienna, 1565)

was appointed second organist at St Mark's, Venice, in 1541. It was decided, on the grounds of the composition he submitted, 'che uno maestro Iachet Fiamengo sia il più eccellente de tutti li altri compositori in quella arte' (that one master Iachet, from Flanders, is the most excellent of all composers in that art).* After a visit to his home country in

---

* See R. Lenaerts, 'La Chapelle de Saint-Marc à Venise sous Adriaen Willaert (1527–1562)', *Bulletin de l'Institut Historique Belge de Rome*, 19 (1938), 230.

1550, he travelled back to Venice by way of Vienna. There he stayed at the court of Archduke Ferdinand, who succeeded in persuading him to enter his service. Venetian attempts to make Buus resume his work in St Mark's came to nothing.

Buus's vocal output consists of about thirty motets and over fifty chansons. His historical importance, however, lies more in the field of instrumental music. Although only eighteen ricercars have been preserved, these pieces represent as important stage in the development of instrumental ensemble writing.

CICONIA [C(h)ywogne], Johannes (*b* Liège, *c*.1335 /*c*.1370; *d* Padua, 1411)

poses a difficult problem for music historians on account of his biography. The question of when the composer was born is not easily answered. Do the 'early' documents from Liège and Avignon which speak of one Johannes Ciconia refer to the composer? Or was the composer Johannes Ciconia who died in Padua in 1411 the son of one Johannes Ciconia, who was born in Liège about 1335?* While no decision can be made about the year of the composer's birth, it is still possible that Ciconia made his way to Italy by way of Avignon as the travelling companion of Cardinal Albornoz in 1358. Shortly before the turn of the century Ciconia wrote some ceremonial compositions for Padua, the town where in any case he finally went to reside in 1402: these mark the beginning of the period in which the Netherlanders took a dominant role in Italian musical life. As cantor at the cathedral Ciconia also maintained contacts with the University of Padua. He wrote some important musicological treatises. After his death his compositions were disseminated as far afield as Germany and Poland.

Ciconia left a varied *œuvre*. Among his sacred compositions there are eleven settings of the Gloria and Credo, the majority of them in formal pairs, with or without tropes. Five of the ceremonial motets are isoperiodic, like *Albane misse celitus*, while nine, such as *O Padua sidus praeclarum*, are freely composed; in most of these two different texts are sung at the same time. His secular compositions, including the famous *O rosa bella*, have texts in Italian (eighteen works) and French (three), and are written in the form of the ballata, the madrigal, and the virelai. Finally, two puzzle canons may be mentioned.

---

* For a résumé of the various hypotheses see P. van Nevel, *Johannes Ciconia (ca.1370–1411). Een muzikaal-historische situering* (Berchem, 1981).

CLEMENS [Clement] (NON PAPA), Jacobus (*b* between *c.*1510 and 1515; *d* 1555 or 1556)

came from the province of either South Holland, Zeeland, or Flanders. His name is mentioned for the first time in 1544, in the chapter archives of the Church of St Donatian in Bruges, as 'Jacobus Clement Pbro' (*Presbytero*: priest). He was appointed a singer in the same year. His unusual sobriquet 'non Papa', which was probably given him by way of a joke, first appears in 1546 in the *Motecta quinis [five] vocibus Clemens non Papa* ... published by Susato. It is possible that in 1545 Clemens became the director of the choir at the court of Philip of Croy, Duke of Aerschot and a general of Charles V. The texts of some of his motets pay homage to the emperor. The composer also worked in 's-Hertogenbosch at the invitation of the Illustre Lieve Vrouwe Broederschap, and possibly in Ypres. Connections with Leiden and Dordrecht can also be discerned in his compositions. Clemens's last work was the motet *Hic est vere martyr*; the text, which is on the subject of martyrdom, has been connected with the Spanish Inquisition.

Clemens's *œuvre* is extensive: his sacred music includes fifteen Masses, two Mass sections, about 233 motets, two Magnificat cycles, and 159 *Souterliedekens* and canticles. With the exception of his Requiem and a Mass in honour of the patron saint of St Donatian in Bruges, *Gaude lux Donatiane*, all his Masses are based on a motet or chanson. On three occasions he took one of his own compositions as his starting-point, and he used two each by Manchicourt, Hellinck, and the French composer Claudin de Sermisy. Many of his motets and one Magnificat cycle (which includes settings in all the eight church modes) have survived in the so-called Leiden choirbooks. The texts of his motets are generally liturgical or biblical, as in the case of his *Fremuit spiritu Jesus*. The three-part *Souterliedekens* are the earliest polyphonic settings of Dutch metrical psalms. Apart from almost ninety chansons, seven secular songs on Dutch texts have survived by Clemens, for example *O Venus schoon*. The subject-matter is often love or drink. His music was widely disseminated, and was even performed by the Utraquists in Bohemia in the sixteenth century.

COMPÈRE, Loyset (*b c.*1445; *d* St Quentin, 1518)

came from Artois or Hainault. From 1474 to 1477 he was a member of the court chapel of Galeazzo Maria Sforza in Milan, and thus numbered

Josquin and Gaspar van Weerbecke among his colleagues. From 1486
his name appears as 'chantre ordinaire' in the payrolls of the French
court. In 1494 he was granted French nationality by Charles VIII. The
king's campaign against Italy took Compère to Casale Monferrato,
where a son of Ercole d'Este tried to acquire compositions from him for
the Ferrara court, and then to Rome. He appears later as a composer in
Cambrai and Douai, where he held distinguished positions, possibly on
account of his degree in canon and civil law. At the same time he
maintained contacts with the royal court. He spent the last years of his
life as a canon in St Quentin.

Besides some Mass sections, Compère's Mass production comprises
two complete Masses and three motet cycles for the Ambrosian liturgy.
His *Missa Galeazescha* belongs to this latter category. Compère also wrote
some polyphonic settings of the Magnificat for Vespers. Among his sixteen motets there are two written for state occasions. His best-known
motet is the early 'singers' prayer', *Omnium bonorum plena*. His secular
music includes about fifty chansons, five of which combine French and
Latin texts, as well as a couple of Italian *frottole*.

CRECQUILLON, Thomas (*b* between *c*.1480 and 1500; *d* ?Béthune, 1557)

According to certain documents (including some from 1540), he was
maître de chapelle at the court of Charles V; according to a document of
1547, however, he was a singer. It is naturally possible that he was
demoted in 1547, but he also may have succeeded Gombert as master of
the choirboys, while Cornelis Canis held the position of chief master of
the chapel. Crecquillon held prebends from Dendermonde and Béthune,
where he was a canon from 1555.

Crecquillon's music has been preserved in a large number of sixteenth-
century collections. His church music includes twelve Masses and over a
hundred motets. Parody is his favourite compositional technique, and on
five occasions he took one of his own motets or chansons as a basis.
Only the *Missa kain [Adler] in der Welt so schön* is based on a monophonic
song. His motets are mainly paraliturgical, including a large number of
ceremonial motets. He wrote three laments for members of the imperial
court, including Maximilian of Buren, general to Charles V, and there
are two motets in honour of the emperor himself. No Netherlands
composer left more chansons than Crecquillon. Besides five *chansons
spirituelles*, he set more than 200 secular texts. Susato's third book of
chansons consists almost exclusively of works by this composer. Many of

his chansons are also found in arrangements for lute: *Ung gay bergier* was among the most popular songs of the sixteenth century.

73
76

Danckerts, Ghiselin (*b* Tholen, *c.*1510; *d* 1565 or later)

From 1538 to 1565 he was a singer, and also secretary and administrator, of the Sistine Chapel in Rome, where great composers such as Costanzo Festa, Morales, Arcadelt, and Palestrina were among his colleagues. In 1551 he joined with the Spaniard Escobedo to form the jury in the famous dispute between Nicola Vicentino and Vicente Lusitano about the role of chromaticism; he wrote his *Trattato* in connection with this event. In 1565 he was described as a man 'without voice, exceedingly rich, given to women and inefficient'. From 1554 he held a prebend in Lille.

The surviving works of Danckerts comprise no more than a few motets, madrigals, and puzzle canons. His importance lies mainly in the field of music theory. As a theorist he adopted a conservative standpoint, but his statements concerning the so-called *generi inusitati* show a perfect combination of theory and practice in the treatment of chromaticism.

5
15
17
22
23
27
30
31
34–5
36
39
43
59
60–2
63–4
70
89
96–8
103
128–9
133
137

Dufay [du Fay], Guillaume (*b* ?Cambrai, 1397 or 1398; *d* Cambrai, 1474)

is regarded as the greatest composer of the first half of the fifteenth century. His name appears for the first time in 1409 in a list of choirboys at the cathedral in Cambrai. He probably came into contact with Carlo Malatesta at the Council of Constance (1414–18); he was present at the Malatesta court in Rimini at the beginning of the 1420s. Dufay possibly travelled back to France in about 1423, and in 1426 he again bade farewell to the country with the chanson *Adieu ces bons vins de Lannoys*. In 1428 he went by way of Bologna, where he perhaps wrote his *Missa Sancti Jacobi*, to Rome; he worked as a member of the papal chapel there until 1437. His contacts with the d'Este family in Ferrara and the Duke of Savoy date from this period. As early as 1434 Dufay held a prebend from St Donatian's Church in Bruges, and two years later he was named a canon of Cambrai (without residential duties), while in 1446 he became a canon at St Waudru's Church in Mons. With the exception of eight years (1451–8) which he spent in Chambéry, the composer lived for the second half of his life in the episcopal see of Cambrai. Here he carried out various functions at the cathedral and acquired great fame. Dufay's own Requiem was performed at his funeral.

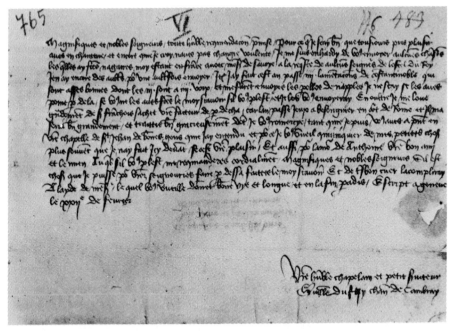

FIG. 38. An autograph letter from Guillaume Dufay to Piero and Giovanni de' Medici in Florence, in which the composer informs them that he has sent some chansons and that he composed four *Lamentacions de Constantinoble* in the previous year (see p. 97). Florence, Archivio di Stato.

Dufay's *œuvre* is greater and more diverse than that of any earlier composer. Leaving aside the 'doubtful' Masses which have been attributed to him, seven complete settings of the Mass Ordinary and almost forty Mass sections by him are known. Some of the sections have survived in distinct pairs, and their texts are often troped. Two of the Masses, *Resvelliés vous* and *Se la face ay pale* are associated musically with Dufay's ballades of the same name. The *Missa Ave regina celorum* was probably written for the dedication of the cathedral in Cambrai in 1472. Besides parts of the Mass Propers for several feasts, including those of St James and St Anthony of Padua, it is possible that Dufay composed eleven complete cycles of Propers. The eight sequences, such as *Veni Sancte Spiritus* and *Victimae paschali laudes*, also belong to this category. His liturgical music moreover includes more than twenty hymn settings, four Magnificats, and fourteen antiphons; he set the texts 'Alma redemptoris mater' and 'Ave regina celorum' more than once. Dufay's motets can be divided into two groups: the thirteen ceremonial motets, which include *Nuper rosarum flores* for the dedication of the cathedral in Florence (these have isoperiodic structures), and the six 'song' motets, which include the three-voice *Flos florum*. The secular music comprises a great number of French chansons: ten ballades, sixty-five rondeaux, and some bergerettes and free compositions. *O tres piteulx | Omnes amici eius*, a lament on the fall of Constantinople (1453), belongs to the last category. Dufay also set one Latin secular text and eight Italian poems, including Petrarch's canzone 'Vergine bella'.

53
99
148   FÉVIN, Antoine de (*b* ?Arras, *c.*1470; *d* Blois, 1511 or 1512)

was associated with the court of Louis XII from 1507 as a singer in Orléans and Blois. In 1547 Glarean called him a 'symphoneta aurelia-nensis' (composer from Orléans) and 'felix Jodoci aemulator' (fruitful follower of Josquin). Antoine was honoured together with his possible brother Robert (as 'the noble brothers') and a number of other compo-sers in the motet *Mater floreat florescat* by Pierre Moulu. On his death the French composer Jean Mouton wrote the chanson *Qui ne regrettroit le gentil fevin?*

Févin's church music is the most important part of his *œuvre*, including ten Masses, three Magnificats, three Lamentations settings, and fifteen motets. Besides parody Masses on motets by Josquin (*Ave Maria ... virgo serena* and *Mente tota*) and himself, there are some Masses in which a chant functions as a *cantus prius factus*. The text of the motet *Gaude, Francorum regia corona* refers to a celebration at the French court. His seventeen chansons are mainly based on French folksongs.

99   GASCONGNE, Mathieu

was 'magister' and priest in the diocese of Cambrai in 1518. It is reason-able to date his musical activity to the period between about 1500 and 1530 on the basis of his surviving music. He possibly had a particular relationship with the French court, since several of his motets allude to François I. In one of his theoretical treatises, Gioseffo Zarlino counted the composer among the 'buoni antichi' together with Ockeghem, Josquin, and Mouton.

Gascongne's church music consists of about twenty motets and eight Masses, assuming that the 'Johannes Gascoing' to whom the *Missa Myn herte heeft altyt verlanghen* is attributed may be identified with Mathieu. In this Mass the song of the same name by La Rue is parodied, as in the *Missa Pourquoi non*. The compositions of Josquin and Févin also provided models for Masses by Gascongne. Among his motets there are two Magnificat settings and a work to a text from the Song of Songs, *Nigra sum*. His fifteen chansons are mainly for three voices; their choices of text show them to belong to the genre of the *chanson rustique*.

GHISELIN [VERBONNET], Johannes

was recorded as 'da Piccardia' and 'fiamengo' in Florence (1493) and Ferrara (1502) respectively. A letter from the Ferrarese ambassador in France in 1501 notes that Ghiselin was a singer in the chapel of the French king. During his time in the service of Ercole d'Este he was responsible, among other things, for the recruitment of singers in France. At the same time he sent compositions by Josquin from France to the d'Este court, and at Ercole's request accompanied the composer on his journey to Ferrara in 1503. A year later he seems also to have accompanied Obrecht when the latter likewise moved to Ferrara from Bergen op Zoom. As far as is known Ghiselin's last place of residence was Bergen op Zoom. He may certainly be regarded as an important contemporary of Josquin, since Petrucci published a collection of his Masses as early as 1503; moreover, he was named in Cretin's lament on the death of Ockeghem (see p. 130), and treated with high regard in several theoretical treatises. It is not certain whether the name Ghiselin was a second Christian name or a nickname indicating his place of origin (Ghislain, Ghislenghien). The signature 'Johannes Ghiselin alias Verbonnet' shows that in any case the many attributions to 'Verbonnet' and 'Ghiselin' refer to the same composer.

Eight Masses by Ghiselin are known, one of which has survived incomplete. While the *Missa De les armes* is built on a sequence of six notes, Ghiselin based his other Masses on chansons by Busnois, Dufay, himself (*Missa Ghy syt die werste boven al*), and others. Seven of his twelve motets are dedicated to Mary. The *Inviolata* and *Regina coeli* have as their *cantus prius factus* the tenor from Binchois's chanson *Comme femme desconfortée*. Besides three instrumental pieces, including the well-known *La Alfonsina*, Ghiselin's secular œuvre contains twelve chansons, four Dutch songs and one Italian, and a setting of Virgil's 'Dulces exuviae'.

GOMBERT, Nicolas (*b c.*1495; *d c.*1560)

probably came from Southern Flanders. His name appears for the first time in 1526 in a list of prebends signed by Charles V in Granada; as a singer he then held prebends in Courtrai and Béthune, among other

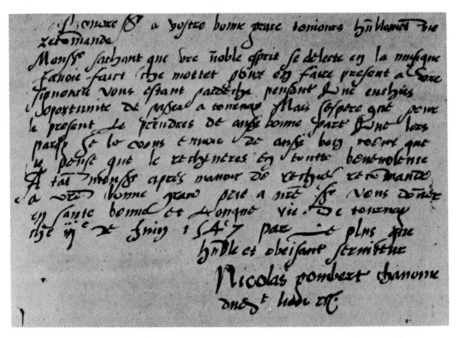

FIG. 39. An autograph letter of homage from Nicolas Gombert to Ferrante Gonzaga, a general of Charles V. The composer sent a motet with the letter. New York, Pierpont Morgan Library.

places. In 1529 the composer was appointed master of the choirboys at the imperial court, a post he held at least until 1537. He accompanied the emperor on his journeys to Spain, Italy, Germany, and the Low Countries. In 1534 Gombert was named a canon (without residential duties) of the cathedral in Tournai. There is evidence of misdemeanours with a choirboy in Spain, and he was sentenced to the galleys. This punishment was lifted in return for compositions which he sent to Charles.* The Spanish theorist Juan Bermudo praises the music of the 'profundo Gomberto'.

Gombert left a large number of works. His church music includes eleven Masses, more than 160 motets, and eight Magnificat cycles. On two occasions he took a chant as the basis for a Mass, for instance in the *Missa Tempore Paschali*. The six-part texture of this work is increased in the Credo to eight voices and in the Agnus Dei to twelve. The other

* See C. Miller, 'Jerome Cardan on Gombert, Phinot, and Carpentras', *The Musical Quarterly*, 58 (1972), 412–19.

Masses are based on motets (two of his own) and chansons (by Bauld-eweyn, Pipelare, and Josquin among others). The *Missa Sur tous regretz* has also survived under the title *Missa A la incoronation*, and was possibly performed at the coronation of Charles V as Emperor in Bologna in 1530. Some of Gombert's motets are connected with festivals at the Habsburg court. The sacred motets take their texts mainly from the Bible. About a quarter are dedicated to the Virgin; Gombert set the anti-phon 'Regina coeli' as many as three times, for four, ten, and twelve voices respectively. His secular music includes more than seventy chan-sons, among which the arrangements of chansons by Josquin and Clément Janequin are notable. A Spanish *canción* and an Italian madrigal witness to his period in the south.

HAYNE VAN GHIZEGHEM (*b* ?Gijzegem, *c*.1445; *d* 1472–97)

was entrusted to the care of Constans Breuwe (Constans van Langbroek or Trecht) by the Count of Charolais (the future Charles the Bold) in 1456. In 1467 Hayne appears on the list of singers in the service of Charles the Bold. In the anonymous rondeau *La plus grand chiere de jamais* it is stated that Hayne and the English composer Robert Morton, who was also active at the Burgundian court, were both in Cambrai in 1468. It is not certain whether Hayne was still in the service of the French King after the battle near Beauvais in 1472. Hayne is named in Cretin's lament on the death of Ockeghem as one of the musicians who welcome the aged musician to paradise.

Hayne's known works consist entirely of chansons. Of the twenty which are attributed to him, only eleven are definitely his work; these are all rondeaux. *Allez regretz* and *De tous biens plaine* were exceptionally popular, and formed the basis of numerous other compositions.

HELLINCK, Lupus [Wulfaert] (*b c*.1496; *d* Bruges, 1541)

was the son of Johannes Hellinck of the diocese of Utrecht. In 1505 he became a choirboy at St Donatian in Bruges; after studying for the priesthood he gained a position at the same church. In 1521 Hellinck entered the service of the Church of Our Lady in Bruges as 'phonascus' (precentor). Two years later he obtained a similar post at St Donatian, and he probably carried out these duties until his death. The composer enjoyed great fame in his own town, and one writer about music from Bruges referred to him as 'Lupus noster Hellinc'. The fact that one of his colleagues in Cambrai was called Johannes Lupi (see 'Lupi' below) was the cause of great confusion which even involved the Antwerp music printer Susato: he published a book of Masses in 1545 in which he presents the two composers as one: 'Ioan. Lupo hellingo'.

On account of this confusion it is difficult to outline Hellinck's *œuvre* clearly. Thirteen parody Masses are ascribed to him; in four of these he chose a motet by Jean Richafort of Hainault as his point of departure, while two are built on his own motets. Like Josquin he based a Mass on Brumel's motet *Mater patris*. *Panis quem ego dabo* is the best-known of his fifteen motets, because of the parody Masses by Clemens non Papa and Palestrina. Hellinck's eleven German chorales were published posthumously in Wittenberg. Chansons and Dutch songs, such as *Aenhoert al myn geclach*, constitute his ten or so secular compositions.

ISAAC, Heinrich [Arrigo il Tedesco] (*b c*.1450; *d* Florence, 1517)

came from Flanders. His name appears for the first time in an Innsbruck document dated 1484. In that year he apparently passed through the town on his way to Florence, where he entered the service of the Medici in 1485. He was registered under the name Arrigo da Fiandra as a singer in the cathedral. His marriage to a Florentine lady, arranged by Lorenzo the Magnificent himself, strengthened his connection with the city. One year after the death of Lorenzo (1492) the Cantori di San Giovanni, to which Isaac belonged, were disbanded. Maximilian I came in contact with the composer during a visit to North Italy in 1496, and this led to Isaac's lengthy period of service at the Habsburg court. In 1497 'Hainrich Ysackh' was appointed court composer by imperial decree. Despite this connection Isaac undertook regular journeys to Florence. He also visited Torgau, Innsbruck, Augsburg, Nuremberg, and Constance on a number of occasions; he composed part of the famous *Choralis constantinus* for the latter city. A letter of 2 September 1502 proves that Isaac was the preferred candidate as court composer to Ercole d'Este (see 'Josquin' below). From 1514 he lived once again in Florence, maintaining only a formal relationship with Maximilian. At the same time he received an honorarium from the emperor and a pension from the city of Florence. This pension was granted at the request of Leo X, the son of Lorenzo and a former pupil of Isaac. Three wills made by Isaac have been preserved.

Isaac, who was a quick worker, left an unusually large number of compositions, and their Netherlandish, Italian, and German stylistic traits

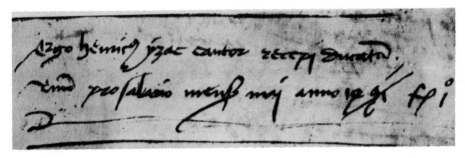

FIG. 40. A receipt written by Heinrich Isaac for his salary as a singer at the Annunziata Church in Florence: 'ego henricus yzac cantor recepj ducatum unum pro salario mensis mai anno 1491'. Florence, Archivio di Stato.

lend them a cosmopolitan character. His church music includes thirty-six settings of the Ordinary of the Mass, and almost a hundred settings of the Proper. The Propers, called *Choralis constantinus*, set the texts for the Sundays of the Church year and the great feasts, including those of Mary and a number of saints. As in half of his settings of the Ordinary of the Mass, chants form the basis of these compositions. But many secular song melodies also found their way into Isaac's Masses. In his *Missa Carminum* he adapted at least nine different folk melodies, including the famous 'Innsbruck, ich muss dich lassen'. Four- and six-part versions of his *Missa Comment peult avoir joye* have survived. The *Missa Een vrolic wesenn* is based on a three-part song by the Antwerp composer Jacobus Barbireau. Among his fifty-odd motets there is a setting of Politian's lament on the death of Lorenzo de' Medici, 'Quis dabit capiti meo aquam', and a *Virgo prudentissima* written for Maximilian. Isaac's secular music includes about eighty vocal and instrumental arrangements of Dutch, French, Italian, and German songs.

JOHANNES DE LIMBURGIA

possibly came from the small town of Limburg near Verviers. Shortly after 1400 he gained the position of chaplain at the Church of St John the Evangelist in Liège, and in 1408 he was named 'bastonarius' (chief singer with a baton). His complete *œuvre* is found in an Italian manuscript (Bologna Q15), and some of his ceremonial motets were written for Venice, Padua, and Vicenza; it is therefore almost certain that he worked in northern Italy from about 1430. In 1436 the composer was named a canon at the Church of Our Lady in Huy.

The forty compositions by Johannes de Limburgia are all religious. He composed one complete Mass Ordinary and some individual sections; his music for the office comprises five Magnificat settings and six hymns. His *œuvre* also includes some strophic, *lauda*-like pieces, and motets of various kinds such as occasional pieces, Marian motets, and settings of texts from the Song of Songs (for example, *Tota pulchra es*).

JOSQUIN DES PREZ [Desprez, Jodocus Pratensis]
(*b* c.1440; *d* Condé-sur-l'Escaut, 1521)

was the greatest composer of his generation. He came from Vermandois, a county in the former province of Picardy. The first mention of his name ('Judocho de frantia biscantori') is found in 1459 in Milan, where he was active as a singer at the cathedral, a post he held until 1472. In 1474 he appears on a payroll of the 'cantori di capella' in the service of the Milanese Duke Galeazzo Maria Sforza. Alexander Agricola, Gaspar van Weerbecke, Johannes Martini, and Loyset Compère were among his colleagues. After Galeazzo's murder (1476), Josquin possibly entered the service of his brother Ascanio, and in 1484, when Ascanio became a cardinal, Josquin was in Rome. From 1486 to 1494 Josquin was in any case in the service of the papal chapel under Innocent VIII and Alexander VI. Weerbecke and Marbrianus de Orto were also members of this chapel. Since the payrolls for the period 1495 to 1500 are lost, Josquin's activities during those years are not known. Between 1501 and 1503 he was possibly at the French court: some of his compositions and his contact with Johannes Ghiselin during this period suggest this. But it is not impossible that he already had a particular relationship with Ercole d'Este. A letter from the Ferrarese envoy at the French court proves that Philip the Fair, during his visit to Blois in 1501, requested Louis XII to lend him Josquin for his journey to Spain. Pierre de la Rue and Alexander Agricola were already among his retinue. Josquin arrived in Ferrara in 1503 by way of Lyons. A letter from Ercole's courtier Gian da Artiganova dated 1502 undoubtedly convinced the Duke to offer Josquin the position of *maestro di cappella*:

in my opinion he [Isaac] is very fit to serve Your Excellency, much more than Josquin, since he can get on well with his colleagues, and will write new pieces more often. It is true that Josquin composes better, but he does it only when he wishes to, not when someone else wishes him to, and he demands 200 ducats as salary while Isaac would settle for 120. May Your Excellency decide what you consider best . . .

IOSQVINVS PRATENSIS.

FIG. 41. Portrait of Josquin des Prez. This woodcut is in Petrus Opmeer's *Opus chronographicum orbis universi* (Antwerp, 1611), and was produced, indirectly, after a painted portrait which was hung in St Gudule's Church in Brussels after his death, but which was destroyed by fire in 1542 (see also p. 69).

In Ferrara the famous psalm motet *Miserere* was written at Ercole's request. The plague epidemic of 1503 forced Josquin to end his stay. In 1504 he was in Condé, where he was appointed as a canon. From here the composer perhaps maintained contact with the court of Margaret of Austria in Malines: like Charles V, the regent had some of Josquin's chansons in her possession. Very little is known of Josquin's last years. The inscription on his gravestone contained the following lines: 'Chy gist Sire Josse despres Preuost de cheens fut jadis . . . .' (Here lies Master Josse Despres. He was once a canon at Condé . . .).

166
167
170
173
174
181

Josquin's *œuvre* is extensive, but at the same time difficult to determine exactly. The number of compositions attributed to him in at least one source can be established with considerable accuracy: forty-one Masses and Mass sections, 160 motets, and a hundred secular works. None the less at least a third of these 300 compositions are not authentic. Some of the Masses, such as the *Missa Pange lingua*, are based on chant; others, such as the two *L'homme armé* Masses, on a secular monophonic song; and others on compositions from earlier composers, like Ockeghem, Busnois, and Hayne van Ghizeghem. Josquin used an ostinato motif as the basic element in the Masses *La sol fa re mi* and *Hercules dux Ferrarie*. The numerous motets are best classified according to their texts: more than half take their texts from the Bible, and among these the so-called psalm motets hold an important place. He also set many texts of prayers in honour of Christ and Mary, from both liturgical and devotional sources. Finally, a small number are based on other texts. The rich diversity of ideas contained in this repertoire of texts is expressed in an inimitable way in his music: the serene *Ave Maria . . . virgo* contrasts with the dramatic *Stabat mater*; the touching biblical lament *Planxit autem David* stands beside the cool, humanistic ode *Ut Phoebi radiis*, and the five-part psalm of mourning, *De profundis clamavi*, shows a strong contrast with the cheerful *Laudate, pueri, Dominum*. His secular works consist for the most part of chansons, but Josquin also set a few Italian texts and passages from Virgil's *Aeneid*. *Adieu mes amours*, *Mille regretz*, and *Nymphes des bois* may be considered some of his most famous chansons. His instrumental pieces include a four-part virtuoso arrangement of Hayne's *De tous biens plaine*.

15
25–6

KERLE, Jacobus de (*b* Ypres, 1531 or 1532; *d* Prague, 1591)

was appointed master of the choirboys in Orvieto as early as 1555, and shortly afterwards he was named cathedral organist and town carilloneur. After a stay in Venice, where his Vesper psalms appeared in print, he met Cardinal Otto Truchsess, who commissioned him to compose the *Preces speciales* for the Council of Trent. Kerle made some journeys in the retinue of the cardinal, including visits to Spain and Germany. In 1565 he was back in Ypres. However, he directed the chapel there for only a short while, since he was excommunicated in 1567. He then went to Augsburg by way of Rome. In 1574 he exchanged the prebend which he had obtained there for one at the cathedral in Cambrai, where he was named a member of the chapter in 1579. The next moves in his uncertain career were to Cologne and Augsburg in 1582. In the following year he settled in Prague as a singer in the imperial court chapel.

Except for two books of madrigals (now lost) and three other secular compositions, Kerle wrote only church music. His corpus of liturgical music consists of three books containing fourteen Masses, including a Requiem, twenty-five hymns, sixteen Magnificats, and twenty psalms. In addition, about a hundred motets by him are known. However, Kerle's *Preces speciales* have contributed the most substantially to his renown. The texts of these works are easily understandable despite the polyphonic character of the music; it is not entirely unthinkable that they might have enabled the composer to avert the abolition of polyphonic music from the Roman Catholic liturgy.

LA HÈLE, George de (*b* Antwerp, 1547; *d* Madrid, 1586)

gained his instruction as a choirboy in the Church of Our Lady in Antwerp, and at the early age of 13 he went to Madrid, where he served under Pierre de Manchicourt in the chapel of Philip II. After some years of study at the University of Alcalá, La Hèle travelled back to the north in 1570 to study theology in Louvain. Two years later he obtained the post of *kapelmeester* at St Rombold's Church in Malines; in 1574 he exchanged this post for the same position at the cathedral in Tournai. Shortly after 1580 La Hèle became master of Philip II's chapel in Madrid. Under his direction the repertoire broadened to include works by Clemens non Papa and others. He married shortly before his death, and thus lost the prebends which Philip had obtained for him.

Only a few compositions by La Hèle have been preserved. This is probably the result of the fire which swept through the Spanish royal chapel in 1734. As a composer La Hèle has mainly been remembered for the monumental edition of his eight Masses, which was printed on Plantin's presses in Antwerp in 1578. The enormous format of the edition (58 × 38 cm.) and Plantin's craftsmanship together created a unique music print (see Fig. 42). The compositions belong to the genre of the parody Mass, using as their models two motets by Josquin (including *Benedicta es*), four by Lasso (including *Fremuit spiritu Jesus*), and one each by Crecquillon and Rore.

FIG. 42. Title-page of the monumental edition of George de la Hèle's eight Masses, produced by Christoffel Plantin in 1578. The same woodcut was also used for other editions, including a collection of Masses by Philippe de Monte.

Lantins, Arnold de and Hugo de

were from the same family, and possibly came from the diocese of Liège. Their compositional activity occurred between 1420 and 1430, and for the most part their music survives in north Italian manuscripts. In 1428 Arnold was in Venice, and in 1431 he was (together with Dufay) a member of the papal chapel. Hugo wrote a few ceremonial motets which suggest a possible relationship with Venice and the Malatesta family in Rimini. In all probability he too had some contact with Dufay.

The church music of Arnold de Lantins comprises the *Missa Verbum incarnatum* (a cycle which consists of an Introit, Kyrie, Sanctus, and Agnus Dei), three Gloria–Credo pairs, and three motets. His secular *œuvre* consists of two ballades and twelve rondeaux.

Apart from two Gloria settings all the Mass sections attributed to Hugo de Lantins are of doubtful authenticity. Five motets, three ballate, and twelve rondeaux by him have survived.

La Rue [Platensis, de Vico, de Robore, van Straeten], Pierre de [Pierchon] (*b c.*1460; *d* Courtrai, 1518)

was possibly a tenor at the cathedral in Siena in 1482 and from 1483 to 1485. In 1489 he was a singer in 's-Hertogenbosch, where he became a member of the Illustre Lieve Vrouwe Broederschap three years later. In the archives of this confraternity he was named as 'Cantor Romanorum regis'; this indicates that he belonged to the Burgundian court chapel of Maximilian. In 1493 La Rue entered the service of Maximilian's son Philip the Fair, with whom he made two journeys to Spain. After the sudden death of Philip in Burgos in 1506 the composer remained for a while in the chapel of Joan the Mad. Two years later he became a singer in the court chapel of Margaret of Austria in Malines. Margaret cherished a great admiration for La Rue, as can be seen from the many compositions by him which appear in the music manuscripts prepared for the regent's court. In 1516 the composer retired on a pension; he settled in Courtrai, where he was named a canon of the Church of Our Lady.

La Rue assumes an important place among Josquin's contemporaries on account of the extent of his *œuvre* and the high quality of his music. He wrote no fewer than thirty-one Masses and seven Mass sections. Chant frequently forms the starting-point for his liturgical music, as for example in the *Missa paschalis*, the *Missa Ave Maria*, and the Requiem. In his *Missa de septem doloribus* the composer uses a sequence, whose different melodic sections form a cyclic *cantus prius factus* for the five movements. The *Missa Nuncqa fuè pena mayor* is based on the song of the same name by his compatriot Johannes Urrede (= Wrede), who had emigrated to Spain. It is not certain whether the *Missa O gloriosa Margaretha* was written to honour his patroness. His liturgical music also contains seven Magnificats and a setting of the Lamentations; there are no fewer than six settings of the 'Salve regina' among his twenty-odd motets. His secular music comprises about thirty chansons and the Dutch song *Mijn hert altijt heeft verlanghen*. The melancholy atmosphere of court life under Margaret is incomparably expressed in several of La Rue's chansons, such as *Autant en emporte le vent* and *Secretz regretz*.

<table>
<tr><td>viii</td><td rowspan="22">LASSO [Lassus], Orlando di [Orlandus] (*b* Mons, Hainault, 1532; *d* Munich, 1594)

is regarded as the greatest composer of the second half of the sixteenth century. At the age of 13 he was taken to Palermo by Ferrante Gonzaga, one of the generals of Charles V. In the service of Ferrante he came to know the courts of Mantua and Milan (1547–9) as well. About 1550 Lasso accepted a post with Constantino Castrioto in Naples, and there he came into contact with the Accademia de' Sereni. His earliest compositions and the chromatic *Prophetiae Sibyllarum* possibly date from this time: the grotto of the Sibyl of Cumae is near Naples. His next place of residence was Rome, where he received an appointment as *maestro di cappella* at St John Lateran in 1553. In the following year Lasso travelled to Mons to visit his ailing parents. In 1555 he stayed in Antwerp, and established contacts with the publisher Tielman Susato, who printed his first compositions in the same year. The year 1556 was of great importance for the young Lasso: though Philippus de Monte was initially recommended for the post, Lasso was appointed as a tenor at the sumptuous court of Albrecht V of Bavaria in Munich, at the same time as some of his compatriots. Seven years later he was appointed Kapellmeister, a post which he held until his death. Because of Lasso's abilities the Bavarian court chapel was regarded as one of the foremost ensembles in Western Europe in the 1560s. He enjoyed a special position at the court, and his relationship with Albrecht and his son Wilhelm was surely unique: the duke bore great expense in order to preserve the music of his court composer in magnificently illuminated manuscripts and printed editions, while Prince Wilhelm maintained an extensive correspondence with the musician he admired. Some weeks before his death Lasso completed his</td></tr>
<tr><td>8</td></tr>
<tr><td>24</td></tr>
<tr><td>25</td></tr>
<tr><td>37</td></tr>
<tr><td>46</td></tr>
<tr><td>48</td></tr>
<tr><td>53</td></tr>
<tr><td>95</td></tr>
<tr><td>100</td></tr>
<tr><td>102</td></tr>
<tr><td>105</td></tr>
<tr><td>106–8</td></tr>
<tr><td>126</td></tr>
<tr><td>133</td></tr>
<tr><td>134–6</td></tr>
<tr><td>141</td></tr>
<tr><td>157</td></tr>
<tr><td>164</td></tr>
<tr><td>166</td></tr>
<tr><td>171</td></tr>
<tr><td>173</td></tr>
<tr><td>180</td></tr>
<tr><td>181</td></tr>
</table>

FIG. 43. Memorial tablet commemorating Orlando di Lasso. The stone was made from red marble, 84 × 169 cm in size, and a year after the composer's death it was placed in the south wall of the Franciscan Church in Munich. On either side of the coat of arms of Lasso and his wife, the composer is shown kneeling with their nine sons, and his wife with their seven daughters. Munich, Bayerisches Nationalmuseum.

cycle *Lagrime di San Pietro*: this swansong, dedicated to Clement VIII, was the composer's final musical act of devotion. Of the seven children whom Regina Wäckinger bore him, Ferdinand and Rudolph won some fame as composers. On the death of their father they succeeded him in turn as Kapellmeister. In addition they posthumously published a large number of his motets in the *Magnum opus musicum* of 1604.

Lasso's *œuvre* is larger than that of any composer before him. His liturgical music comprises about sixty Masses, 101 Magnificats, about ten settings of the Nunc dimittis (Simeon's song of praise), eighteen Lamentations settings, settings of lessons from the Book of Job, and four Passions. Most of the Mass compositions are based on motets, chansons, and madrigals by Gombert, Willaert, Monte, Lasso himself, and others. But there are Masses based on monophonic songs and freely composed works as well. The three Requiems, the *Missa In te Domine speravi* (on his own motet), the *Jägermesse*, intended for the hunting-season and based on short fanfare motifs, and his last Mass, on Gombert's chanson *Triste depart*, are among his more remarkable compositions. The exceptional popularity of Lasso's Magnificat settings is undoubtedly due partly to their alternatim construction, which makes them particularly

Signature of Orlando di Lasso

suited to liturgical use. In over a quarter of them the composer uses parody technique. The Passions are composed to the accounts of each of the four evangelists, and use the so-called responsorial form: the words of the evangelist and of Christ are recited in chant, while the other parts are set in polyphony. Lasso's capacity to express in music the most diverse moods is best shown in his enormous number of motets—516 in the *Magnum opus musicum* alone. They encompass the emotional setting of Christ's words in *Tristis es anima mea*, the serious tone of the penitential psalms, the majestic splendour of the *Laudate Dominum* and *Tui sunt coeli*, and the quiet resignation in the *Stabat mater*. Among the secular motets there are numerous ceremonial compositions such as *Haec quae ter triplici*, in honour of the three sons of Albrecht V, and also humorous works such as drinking-songs and settings of texts from classical literature (Horace and Virgil). Over 200 Italian madrigals, about 150 French chansons, and 90 German songs form an impressive testimony to the three living languages which the composer—like his predecessor Isaac—had to use in the course of his life. The nature of the texts varies considerably: there are poems by Petrarch, Ariosto, and Tasso, by Ronsard, Marot, and Siant-Gelais, but also many less stylized verses; many of the German songs are witty in nature. His works on German texts also include the *Teutsche geistliche Psalmen* of 1588. These are three-part settings (twenty-five by Lasso and the same number by his son Rudolph) of melodies from a psalter which had been published by the Catholic Caspar Ulenberg six years earlier.

15
88
100
131
152

Lupi [Leleu], Johannes [Jennot] (*b* c.1506; *d* Cambrai, 1539) was a choirboy at the cathedral in Cambrai between 1514 and 1521. In 1522 the chapter gave him a grant to study at the University of Louvain, and until 1526 he was a student in the Faculty of Philosophy there. After his return to Cambrai he was appointed master of the choirboys, and from 1530 he also held the position of vicar. He had to relinquish his office for two years from 1535 as the result of chronic sickness. Though Lupi had not been ordained priest, he was buried in the cathedral nevertheless.

Two Masses by Lupi have survived in Cambrai manuscripts: *Mijn vriendinne* and *Philomena praevia*, the latter on a motet by Richafort. In addition he wrote thirty-seven motets, showing a preference for responsory texts from the liturgy. His Song of Songs motet *Quam pulchra es* was used by Palestrina as the model for a Mass. Lupi's secular music consists of about thirty chansons. Besides melancholy poems he also set light texts such as 'Les fillettes de Tournai' (The girls of Tournai).

MANCHICOURT, Pierre de (*b* Béthune, *c*.1510; *d* Madrid, 1564)

was a choirboy in the cathedral at Arras in 1525. Information on the titlepages of his principal publications show that Manchicourt was in charge of the chapel in the cathedral in Tours in 1539, and in 1545 he had the same responsibilities in the cathedral in Tournai. In 1556 he was a canon in Arras. Three years later he was appointed master of the chapel at the court of Philip II in Madrid.

Manchicourt's church music includes nineteen Masses, one Mass section, and seventy motets. Parody technique is used in most of his Masses. Apart from three of his own motets, he chose works by the French composers Jean Mouton and Claudin de Sermisy as points of departure. The *Missa De domina virgine Maria* and the Requiem are based on chant. The Regent Mary of Hungary had twelve Masses by Manchicourt copied for use in her chapel. Among his motets there are numerous antiphons and responsories; seven texts come from the Song of Songs, and nine are dedicated to Mary. He also wrote three ceremonial motets: *O decus, o patriae lux* honours Cardinal Antoine Perrenot de Granvelle, who became Bishop of Arras in 1537 and in 1559 chief adviser to the Regent Margaret of Parma. Manchicourt's chansons, which number over fifty, are partly melancholy (*Voyant souffrir celle*) and partly cheerful in tone (*Celle qui a fâcheux mari*).

MARTINI, Johannes (*b c*.1440; *d* 1498)

probably came from the Duchy of Brabant. One cannot be certain if the 'Giovanni d'Alemania' who was active at the court of Ercole d'Este in Ferrara in 1473 may be identified with Johannes Martini. In any case,

136 Martini was a singer in the chapel of Galeazzo Maria Sforza in Milan
154 together with Josquin and Compère in 1474. At the end of 1474 he
181 was mentioned in the accounts of the d'Este court as 'Zohane Martini
de Barbante'. The same papers give him the title of 'compositore', a
position which he was to hold until his death. Several documents prove
that Ercole had great respect for him. In 1486, for instance, Martini
accompanied one of the duke's sons on his journey to the court of
Esztergom; during her childhood, Ercole's daughter Isabella took music
lessons with the composer. For Isabella's marriage to Francesco Gon-
gaza of Mantua in 1490 a magnificently illuminated manuscript was produced, in which chansons by Martini form a prominent part.

Martini's sacred works include ten Masses, sixty-seven two- and
three-part psalms, about ten hymns, six Magnificat settings, and some
motets. His *Missa Ma bouche rit* is based on Ockeghem's chanson of the
same name, and the *Missa La martinella* has as its musical basis one of his
own songs. The large number of psalm-settings is remarkable for his
time, the more so since the compositions are scored for two choirs;
Together with his French colleague Johannes Brebis, Martini wrote several other doublechoir works for the office. His secular music includes
the motet *Perfunde coeli rore*, possibly written for Ercole d'Este, about
twenty chansons, seven songs on Italian texts (including *Fortuna desperata*
and *Fortuna d'un gran tempo*), the Dutch song *Groen vink* (which survives
without text), and a few instrumental pieces.

8 MONTE, Philippus de (*b* Malines, 1521; *d* Prague, 1603)

9
46 is reckoned to be the greatest contemporary of Lasso. He probably sang
47 as a choirboy at St Rombold's Church in Malines, and after this training
48 went to Italy. From 1542 to 1551 he was in the service of the Pinelli
68 family in Naples. In 1554 he was in Rome, where his first collection of
94 five-part madrigals appeared. In the same year he travelled to Antwerp
102 and then to England. He remained there for a short time, the only
133 Netherlander connected with the Spanish court chapel of Philip II when
136 the king stayed in England after his marriage to Mary Tudor. Little is
161 known about the subsequent period of Monte's life. Despite the good
171 reference which Vice-Chancellor Seld gave to Albrecht V to recommend
173 him for a post in Munich, Lasso was appointed instead: 'Phillipus de
Monte from Malines . . . is a quiet, withdrawn, and modest person, like
a maiden. He has lived mainly in Italy, speaks Italian as if he had been
born there, as well as Latin, French, and Dutch, and moreover is with-

RIEN SANS PEINE

ÆTATIS SVÆ LXXIII. AN° DÑI 1594

Cernimus excelsum mente, arte, et nomine MONTEM,
Quo Musæ, et Charites constituêre domum.

ADMODV R.ᵈᵉ ⅋ PRÆCLAR.ᵐᵒ VIRO, DÑO PHILIPPO
DE MONTE, BELGÆ, DD. MAX.ᵐⁱ II. ⅋ RVDOL. II.
ROM. IMPP. CHORI MVSICI PRÆFECTO,
Metropol: eccliæ Cameracen. Can.ᶜᵉ et Thesaurario, et c: Raphael
Sadeler obseruant. ergô scalpsit, et dedicauit.   Monachij.
          Cum priuilegiᵒ: Sac: Cæs: M:

FIG. 44. Portrait of Philippus de Monte at 73 years of age. It was
printed from a copper plate engraved by Raphaël Sadeler in Munich
in 1594. Above the portrait is the motto of the composer, and
underneath a Latin play on words that can be translated as follows:
'We see here a mountain, much elevated in spirit, art, and name,
whom the Muses and Graces have taken as their home.'

out a doubt the best composer in the whole country.' His contacts with prominent Italians prove that he worked in Rome in the 1560s. After his compatriot Jacobus Vaet, Kapellmeister at the Viennese court of Maximilian II, died in 1567, Monte was chosen by the emperor as his successor. In 1570 he travelled to the Low Countries to recruit singers for the court chapel. Two years later he was nominated treasurer (without residential obligations) of the cathedral in Cambrai, and in 1577 the chapter promoted him to canon. Monte was also active at the Habsburg court in Vienna and Prague under Maximilian's successor, the art-loving Rudolf II. He directed the court chapel on state occasions; he met Lasso for the last time in 1594 at the Diet of Regensburg. In January 1603 Monte drew up his will, in which he expressed the wish to be buried in St James's Church in Prague.

Monte's works are very numerous. In his thirty-eight Masses he shows a preference for parody technique. The eight Masses published by Plantin in Antwerp are all based on motets, such as *Benedicta es* by Josquin and *Confitebor tibi Domine* by Lasso; but he also took secular music as parody material, for instance his own *Reviens vers moy* and Rore's famous *Anchor che col partire*. His Requiem has been preserved in a manuscript in Vienna. Most of the 250-odd motets by Monte appeared in ten editions of *Cantiones sacrae*, which were printed in Venice. (The sixth book of five-part motets went missing during the Second World War.) He used psalms, antiphons, and other liturgical prayers as his texts. Many motets show signs of the Counter-Reformation in their content. This is also true of his 144 *madrigali spirituali*, which, though outwardly related to their secular equivalents, form a separate genre on account of their texts. The poets of these works include Vittoria Colonna and Petrus Canisius among others. In the field of the secular madrigal Monte showed greater productivity than any of his contemporaries, composing some 1,075 works. Among the texts are poems by Petrarch, Boccaccio, Bembo, and Tasso, and a collection of madrigals on texts from Guarini's *Il pastor fido* appeared in 1600. The fact that several books were reprinted four or five times demonstrates the great popularity of these works. His contribution to the chanson is limited to forty-five compositions; among the most attractive pieces are his settings of sonnets by Ronsard.

36
68–9
148
172

MOULU [Molu], Pierre (*b c.*1480; *d c.*1550)

was a pupil of Josquin, according to Ronsard's *Meslanges des chansons* of 1560. His contrapuntal technique suggests that he came from the Low

Countries. Although nothing is known of his life, the texts of some of his compositions suggest that he was connected with the French court: his chanson *Fiere attropos mauldicte et inhumaine* is a lament on the death in 1514 of Queen Anne of Brittany. In his motet *Mater floreat florescat* Moulu honours twenty-four colleagues, including Dufay, Obrecht, La Rue and Josquin (whom he calls 'incomparable'), and also some musicians active at the French court chapel.

Four Masses by Moulu have survived. The *Missa Missus est Gabriel angelus* has Josquin's motet of the same name as its model; the *Missa Alma redemptoris mater*, also called *Missa A deux visaiges*, can be performed in two ways, with or without rests. Among his twenty-odd motets there are some compositions on secular texts, and the Song of Songs motet *Vulnerasti cor meum* is based on the then popular song 'Dulcis amica Dei'. Well-known melodies of the time appear in the majority of his ten chansons.

NASCO, Jan [Gian] (*b c.*1510; *d* Treviso, 1561)   93

came from Flanders, and in Vicenza entered the service of Paolo Naldi, a captain of the Venetian Republic, as *maestro di cappella*; in 1547 he was appointed musical director of the Accademia Filarmonica in Verona, which had been founded four years previously. One of his duties was to set texts given him by the members. He soon resigned this position on his appointment as *maestro* at the cathedral in Treviso in 1551. Nasco remained there for the rest of his life, though he did not actually end his connection with the academy in Verona. In 1554 he dedicated his first book of four-part madrigals to the members of this academy; the letters which he wrote to them demonstrate his interest in problems concerning the performance of madrigals. It is not improbable that, like Jacquet de Berchem, he maintained close contact with Willaert in Venice. The reprints of his publications prove that his music was popular.

Nasco's works have been confused with those of Maistre Jhan of Ferrara. In so far as his *œuvre* can be determined, it may be described as follows: four Masses (lost during the Second World War); a Lamentations setting and two Passions (one according to St Matthew) which were published posthumously by his widow; about forty motets, psalms, and hymns; and about 115 madrigals and more than twenty *villanelle*.

I

12

14

20–1   was *zangmeester* in Utrecht from 1476 to 1478, during which time

22   Erasmus sang as a choirboy under him. In 1479 he was appointed to the

23   same post at the Capitular Church of St Gertrude in Bergen op Zoom.

25   After his ordination as a priest in 1480, he celebrated his first Mass in

29   Oud-Gastel. From 1481 to 1484 he was master of the choirboys to the

30   Guild of Our Lady in Bergen op Zoom. At the end of 1484 he appears in

32   Cambrai as director of the choir school of the cathedral; when he was

35   dismissed for insufficient achievement a year later, the chapter of St

48   Donatian's Church in Bruges offered him a similar position. He worked

53   for seven years in Bruges, but spent part of 1488 in Bergen op Zoom,

56   and obtained six months' leave for a journey to Ferrara; here he estab-

59   lished his first contact with Duke Ercole d'Este. In 1491, after the death

66   of the master of the choirboys at the Church of Our Lady in Antwerp,

79   Jacobus Barbireau, Obrecht was chosen out of twelve applicants for the

110   position. He carried out this work until 1496. He then remained for

115   a while in Bergen op Zoom, and in 1498 he was appointed to St

120   Donatian's for the second time. His poor health forced him to retire

136   early in 1500. He spent the last years of his life in Bergen op Zoom, but

149

OBRECHT [Hobrecht, Obreth], Jacob (*b* Bergen op Zoom, *c*.1450; *d* Ferrara, 1505)

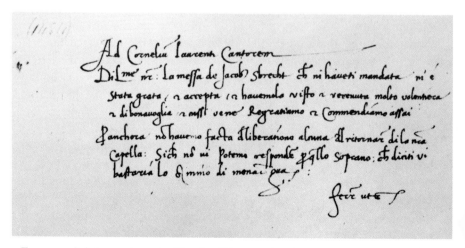

FIG. 45. A letter written by Ercole d'Este to the singer Cornelius Laurenti in 1484 in which the duke confirms having received a Mass by Jacob Obrecht. Modena, Archivio di Stato.

in 1504 he travelled to Ferrara where, like Ercole d'Este, he died of the
plague epidemic in the following year.

Obrecht's church music comprises thirty Masses and about the same number of motets; it is doubtful whether the Passion attributed to him in no fewer than eighteen sources is in fact his work. Almost all his Masses are based on a *cantus prius factus*, either a secular song such as 'Adieu mes amours', a melody from a polyphonic composition such as Hayne van Ghizeghem's *De tous biens plaine*, or a chant such as the responsory 'Sicut spina rosam'. It is notable that in some Masses Obrecht uses several *cantus prius facti*, for example, in the *Missa Diversorum tenorum* (or *Missa Carminum*) and *Missa Schoen lief*. Foremost among his motets are *Parce Domine* and the Marian pieces. In 1488 he wrote a lament on the death of his father. More than half of his almost thirty secular songs have Dutch titles, but their texts have not survived. His only Italian song is *La tortorella*; the other songs have French texts.

OCKEGHEM [Okeghem], Johannes (*b c.*1420; *d* ?Tours, 1497)

possibly came from Okeghem in Eastern Flanders or from Dendermonde. His name appears for the first time in the accounts of the Church of Our Lady in Antwerp for the year 1443. The fact that Ockeghem honoured Binchois with a lament on his death may point to a relationship between the two composers. From 1446 to 1448 he was active in the chapel of Duke Charles I of Bourbon in Moulins. His first contacts with the French court possibly date from this time. In 1452 he entered the service of Charles VII. In January 1454 the king received a volume of music as a New Year's present from his 'premier chapelain'. That Ockeghem enjoyed great respect at court is demonstrated by his princely remuneration and his appointment as treasurer of the Abbey of St Martin in Tours. He maintained his connection with the court chapel under Charles's successor, Louis XI. In 1463 he was appointed to a canonry at Notre Dame in Paris, and two years later he obtained the position of 'maistre de la chapelle de chant du roi'. Apart from a few journeys to Spain and the Low Countries, Ockeghem remained in France until his death. Numerous displays of homage show that he was generally regarded as a great man: Tinctoris dedicated a treatise to him; Isabella d'Este had a canon by him hung in her studio (see Fig. 35); and several poets and composers wrote laments on his death.

Fifteen Masses, one Credo, and about five motets represent Ockeghem's surviving church music; at least four Masses have been lost. His

164
171
172

great technical ability is demonstrated in compositions such as the *Missa Prolationum* and the *Missa Cuiusvis toni*. For his *Missa De plus en plus* he used a melody by Binchois, and in three others he employed his own chanson melodies. Chant forms the basis of his *Missa Caput* and *Missa Ecce ancilla Domini* and the Requiem. His secular music comprises over twenty chansons, most of them rondeaux. These pieces are found in a great number of manuscripts, reflecting their wide dissemination: no fewer than seventeen sources are known of *Ma bouche rit*.

104
154

ORTO [Dujardin], Marbrianus de (*b* c.1460; *d* Nivelles, 1529)

came from the diocese of Tournai and was the illegitimate son of a priest. From 1483 to 1499 he was a singer at the papal chapel, where Josquin was one of his colleagues. Innocent VIII awarded him several prebends. During his period in Rome he was named Dean of St Gertrude's Church in Nivelles; he presented this church with a bronze reliquary. In 1505 he entered the service of Philip the Fair as a singer in his chapel, and he

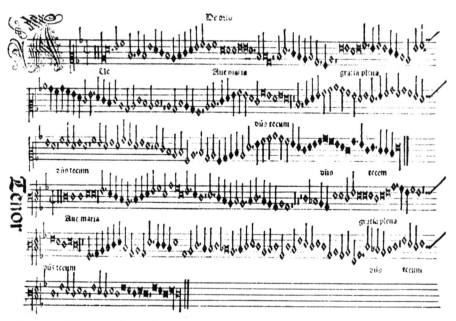

FIG. 46. The superius and tenor of the *Ave Maria* by Marbrianus de Orto. This motet is the opening work of Ottaviano Petrucci's collection *Harmonice musices odhecaton A* (Venice, 1501), the first printed edition of polyphonic music. Bologna, Civico Museo Bibliografico Musicale.

accompanied the king on his journey to Spain as 'premier chapelain'. After Philip's death he occupied the same post for many years under Charles V. In 1510 Orto became a canon at the Church of Our Lady in Antwerp, and three years later he was appointed canon at St Gudule's Church in Brussels.

Orto's *œuvre* consists for the most part of church music: six Masses, in which he preferred to adapt popular songs such as 'La belle se sied' and 'Petite camusette'; one Kyrie, two Credos; six motets, including the *Ave Maria* which Petrucci published as the first composition in his *Odhecaton* (see Fig. 46), the earliest printed publication of polyphonic music in history. His liturgical music also contains a Lamentations setting and two hymns. His surviving secular compositions comprise a Virgil motet, *Dulces exuviae,* and eight chansons. In two of these he cited melodies by Ockeghem.

PEVERNAGE [Bevernage], Andreas (*b* Harelbeke, 1543; *d* Antwerp, 1591)

was *kapelmeester* in St Saviour's Church in Bruges in February 1563, but he obtained a similar position at the Church of Our Lady in Courtrai in the same year. In 1564 he was awarded a prebend at St Willibrord's Church in Hulst. He left Courtrai in 1578 on account of religious and political disturbances and settled in Antwerp, where he was appointed *kapelmeester* of the Church of Our Lady. Apart from being a musician and composer Pevernage was active as an editor: in *Harmonia celeste* (1583), published by Phalèse in Antwerp, he presented over fifty madrigals by Lasso, Monte, Italian composers, and himself among others.

Pevernage's church music comprises six Masses, including *Ego flos campi*, over fifty-five motets, and five so-called picture motets (see p. 74). He also wrote religious pieces on French texts, the thirty-four so-called *chansons spirituelles*. His secular music comprises twenty-five occasional motets, such as *Nympha patris* in honour of Margaret of Parma, seventy-seven chansons (some with texts by Marot), and thirteen madrigals.

PIPELARE, Matthaeus (*b c.*1450; *d c.*1515)

was active in Antwerp before he became 'sangmeester voor die jongen' (singing-master to the boys) of the Illustre Lieve Vrouwe Broederschap in 's-Hertogenbosch, where he remained for two years. He also possibly worked in Ghent: his *Missa Floruit egregius infans Livinus* is dedicated to the patron saint of that town. In a few manuscripts Pipelare's name is made up of the syllables 'pi-pe' and the notes la–re.

Nine Masses, one Credo, and six motets represent Pipelare's surviving church music (two Masses were lost in the Second World War). The *Missa Fors seulement* is based on one of his chansons of the same name, and two chants form the basis of the *Missa Johannes Christe care*. Among his secular works there are four Dutch songs, including a setting of 'Een vrolic wesen', and three chansons.

99
131

PRIORIS [?de Vorste], Johannes (*b* *c*.1460; *d* after 1512)

possibly came from Vorst near Brussels. Though several Vatican manuscripts include compositions by him, one cannot be certain whether the 'D[ominus] Priori organistae', who received a payment from St Peter's in Rome in 1491, may be identified with the composer. In 1503 mention is made of Prioris as *maître de chapelle* of Louis XII. His name also appears in Cretin's lament on the death of Ockeghem and in Moulu's motet in honour of composers (see 'Moulu' above).

Four Masses and a Requiem by Prioris are known. The *Missa Allez regretz* is based on the chanson of the same name by Hayne van Ghizeghem; liturgical chants form the basis of the Requiem, which was reprinted as late as 1553. He wrote almost twenty motets, and, unusually, as many as five settings of the Magnificat. The eight-part *Ave Maria* and the six-part *Da pacem Domine* consist of four and three double canons respectively. Prioris's secular music comprises about ten chansons; the well-known song 'In myne zin' is cited in *Par vous je suis*.

57
66

REGIS [Leroy], Johannes (*b* *c*.1430; *d* ?Soignies, *c*.1495)

was active in Soignies before he was appointed *magister puerorum* at the cathedral in Cambrai and secretary to Dufay. It is not clear if he ever accepted this appointment, since in 1463 he was also reputed to have been singing-master at the Church of Our Lady in Antwerp. Accounts relating to Dufay's will show that Regis was in Cambrai in 1474, and that he was a canon of St Vincent's Church in Soignies at the same time. The composer is mentioned with respect in Compère's 'singers' prayer', and in Cretin's elegy for Ockeghem.

The surviving works of Regis are few in number: two Masses, one Credo, nine motets, and two chansons. The motets frequently contain an appropriate *cantus prius factus*: in the Marian motet *Ave rosa speciosa*,

Johannes Regis Cameraci

The name of Johannes Regis 'of Cambrai' as the composer signed it on the flyleaf of a precious Jewish book of rituals and prayers. Cambrai, Bibliothèque municipale, Ms. 946.

for example, the antiphon 'Beata mater' is heard as a two-part canon in the two tenor parts. The rondeau *S'il vous plaist* appears in the splendid heart-shaped chanson album of Jean de Montchenu.

R EGNART, Jacob (*b* Douai, *c*.1540; *d* Prague, 1599)

69
105
108
180

called himself 'Flandrus' on the title-pages of his publications. In 1577 he was appointed to the court chapel of Archduke Maximilian, the future emperor, which was directed by Jacobus Vaet. After some years in Italy he appears in 1576 in Vienna as a 'tenor and teacher of the choirboys'. In 1579 he was appointed vice-Kapellmeister by Maximilian's successor, Rudolf II, who resided in Prague. His closest colleague was Monte, who succeeded Vaet as Kapellmeister in 1567. In 1582 Regnart accepted an appointment as vice-Kapellmeister at the court of Archduke Ferdinand in Innsbruck; three years later he became Kapellmeister. In 1585 he also received Lasso during his stay in Innsbruck on his way to Loreto. In 1588 Regnart published his *Mariale*, a collection of motets in honour of Mary, written in thanksgiving for recovery from a serious illness. When the court chapel was disbanded on the death of Ferdinand in 1595, the composer travelled back to Prague to resume his work as vice-Kapellmeister.

A substantial amount of music by Regnart has been lost, but the surviving works are nevertheless numerous. The range of material which he used as starting-points for his thirty-six Masses proves to be eclectic: chants, sacred and secular folksongs, motets (there are two Masses on Josquin's *Benedicta es*), madrigals, and chansons (including *Comme la tourterelle* by Monte). The models for eight of his Masses, including *Oeniades Nymphae*, cannot yet be identified. He wrote about 180 motets, one of which, the nine-part angel choius *Justorum animae*, was intended for the play *Speculum vitae humanae*, which was performed in Innsbruck in 1584. Regnart's sacred music also includes a *St Matthew Passion*, a Marian litany, and nine German songs. His secular music comprises four ceremonial motets, and a lament for Vaet, two Latin odes, thirty-five Italian canzoni, and more than a hundred songs with German texts. The popular song *Einsmals in einem tiefen Tal*, in which a cuckoo and a nightingale refer a dispute on the qualities of their voices to arbitration by an ass, belongs to the last category. Another German setting, *Venus, du und dein Kind*, was given a religious text and included in Protestant hymnbooks in the seventeenth century.

RORE, Cypriano de (*b* Ronse, 1515 or 1516; *d* Parma, 1565)

probably went to Italy in the 1530s, and possibly belonged to the group of musicians who were active at St Mark's, Venice, under Willaert. The earliest indication of his presence in Ferrara, where he obtained the position of *maestro di cappella* to the d'Este family, dates from 1547, but it is possible that Rore had been appointed to this position a few years earlier. In 1558 Rore visited his parents in Flanders, and he returned to travelled north. During at least one of these journeys Rore visited the court of Albrecht V in Munich, where his portrait was painted by Mielich. When Ercole II died in 1559, his son Alfonso did not wish to extend Rore's appointment. The composer then made contact with Margaret of Parma in Brussels, and this led to his appointment at the court of her husband, Ottavio Farnese, in Parma. After Willaert's death in 1562 Rore was chosen as his successor. However, the position of *maestro di cappella* at St Mark's soon proved too onerous for him, and in 1564 he returned to Parma.

Rore's church music comprises five Masses, a *St John Passion*, and about eighty motets, eight of which were lost during the Second World War. The *Missa Vivat felix Hercules* is built on a *soggetto cavato*, while in the other Masses parody technique is used, Josquin's compositions appearing twice as models. Among his motets are several psalm-settings. His secular music comprises sixteen motets, about 125 madrigals, and seven chansons. Some of the motets, which include the chromatic ode *Calami sonum*, are based on classical texts. Until 1550 Rore showed a preference for Petrarch's verse, including the famous *Vergine* cycle, in his choice of madrigal texts. His setting of Alfonso d'Avalos's madrigal 'Anchor che

FIG. 47. Portrait of Cypriano de Rore, painted by Hans Mielich. Detail from a miniature. Munich, Bayerische Staatsbibliothek, Mus. Ms. B.

col partire' made this text remarkably popular in the second half of the sixteenth century.

Schuyt, Cornelis (*b* Leiden, 1557; *d* Leiden, 1616)

was probably a choirboy at St Peter's Church in Leiden. At about twenty years of age he travelled to Italy to study with a grant from the town. In 1593 he was appointed second town organist (and assistant to his father), and in that capacity he played alternately at St Peter's and St Pancras's Church. From 1601 Cornelis was first organist at St Peter's.

Schuyt's vocal *œuvre* comprises thirty-six madrigals on Italian texts, including *O Leyda gratiosa*, a eulogy of his home town; sixteen *Hollandsche Madrigalen*, or Dutch madrigals (for three to eight parts, though only three partbooks have survived); the canon *Bewaert Heer Hollandt*, and the so-called picture motet *Domine fiant anima mea*. His instrumental music consists of the collection *Dodeci [twelve] padovane et altretante gagliarde* and two canzonas.

Sweelinck [Swelingh], Jan Pieterszoon (*b* Deventer, 1562; *d* Amsterdam, 1621)

was organist of the Oude Kerk in Amsterdam, like both his father and his son. Though an intervening appointment cannot be ruled out—his father died when Sweelinck was eleven—he had a permanent position from no later than 1580. Sweelinck was employed by the town authorities to give regular public concerts. He also enjoyed great fame as a teacher, and his pupils came from far and near; in North Germany he was even called the 'hamburgischen Organistenmacher'. Apart from short journeys which he made to several cities in the Netherlands and to Antwerp as an expert in organ-building, Sweelinck lived in Amsterdam until his death.

The surviving vocal *œuvre* of Sweelinck comprises 153 psalms, thirty-nine motets, thirty-three chansons, nineteen madrigals, seven canons, and two wedding motets, not including doubtful works. He used the metrical versions of Marot and Bèze for his psalm-settings. One of the most spectacular settings is that of Psalm 150, the eight-part *Or soit loué l'Eternel*. The motets, called *Cantiones sacrae*, are based on texts from the Catholic liturgy and the Scriptures, such as the psalms and the Gospels. A remarkable feature of these compositions is the use of *basso seguente*, the instrumental doubling of the lowest part and the chords it implies.

F I G. 48. Jan Pieterszoon Sweelinck as he was painted by his brother Gerrit in 1606. 'The two inferior *Fingers* shut in, and the other three presented in an eminent posture in the extended *Hand*, is a *speaking* Action, significant to *demand silence*, and *procure audience*', as would be expected from a musician. John Bulwer, *Chironomia: or, The Art of Manuall Rhetorique* (London, 1644), 67. The Hague, Gemeentemuseum.

Among the madrigals there are five arrangements of earlier Italian settings, such as Luca Marenzio's *Liquide perle Amor*. Poems by Ronsard, Marot, and others are used in the chansons. The keyboard music that can be safely ascribed to Sweelinck comprises thirteen fantasias, thirteen toccatas, one prelude, and one ricercar; thirteen sets of variations on religious songs in Latin, Dutch, and German; and twelve variations on secular melodies such as 'Mein junges Leben hat ein End''. He also composed some lute pieces.

<table>
<tr><td>14</td><td rowspan="11">TINCTORIS [Teinturier], Johannes (b Eigenbrakel, c.1435; d ?1511)</td></tr>
</table>

14

25
27
38
70
77–8
120
121
136
142
169

TINCTORIS [Teinturier], Johannes (*b* Eigenbrakel, *c*.1435; *d* ?1511)

is considered the most important Netherlands theorist of the fifteenth century. In 1516 the German humanist Trithemius described Tinctoris in his dictionary of biography and bibliography as 'doctor utriusque juris, maximus mathematicus, summus musicus'. Tinctoris possibly sang in the cathedral at Cambrai under Dufay in 1460. Three years later he was admitted as a student at the University of Orléans, where at the same time he gave singing lessons to the choirboys at the cathedral. He also worked as singing-master in Chartres. About 1472 Tinctoris entered the service of King Ferdinand I of Naples as tutor to his daughter Beatrice. He visited Ferrara in 1479, and also possibly spent some time in Rome; in 1487, on Ferdinand's instructions, he recruited singers at the French court. He held a prebend in Nivelles.

Besides his musical *œuvre*, which comprises five Masses, a Lamentations setting, four motets, eight chansons, and instrumental pieces, Tinctoris left no less than twelve theoretical treatises. Two of these were published during his life, including the *Terminorum musicae diffinitorium* of about 1475, which contains 299 terms and is the oldest printed dictionary of music. Three other writings treat several aspects of mensural notation. The comprehensive *Liber de arte contrapuncti* has more than fifty chapters dedicated to the teaching of composition. Many of the musical examples in the treatises come from the works of his Netherlands contemporaries.

69
104
166
173
174

VAET, Jacobus (*b* Harelbeke, *c*.1529; *d* Vienna, 1567)

sang as a choirboy in the Church of Our Lady in Courtrai. In 1547 he was admitted as a student at the University of Louvain. Three years later he appears to have been a tenor in the chapel of Charles V. It is possible that Vaet went to Vienna in 1553 at the invitation of his compatrio' Pieter Maessens, who was Kapellmeister at the court of Ferdinand I or

FIG. 49. The motet *Qui operatus est Petro* by Jacobus Vaet. The composition was printed on parchment in large format by Raphaël Hofhalter of Vienna in 1560 and dedicated to his patron. Five of the six parts are notated. The prayer 'Sancte Petre, ora pro nobis; Sancte Paule, ora pro nobis' (on the upper systems) must be sung by two parts; Peter's key and Paul's sword show the starting-points for the performance of the parts, as explained in the Latin motto: one voice sings the melody from the beginning to the end, the other starts at the end. Vienna, Österreichische Nationalbibliothek.

Habsburg. In the following years he became Kapellmeister to Ferdinand's son Maximilian. When Maximilian succeeded his father in 1564, Vaet was promoted to Kapellmeister to the emperor. On his death the composer was commemorated in elegies by many colleagues, including one by his pupil Jacob Regnart, *Defunctum charites Vaetem*.

Vaet's church music comprises nine Masses, about eighty motets, and eight Magnificat settings. In all the Masses—and even in a number of motets—he uses parody technique. Apart from the motet *Ego flos campi* by Clemens non Papa, Vaet regularly employed his own works as the musical starting-points for new compositions. The structure of the *Missa Tityre, tu patulae* comprises not only the motet of that name by Lasso, but also Vaet's own motet *Vitam quae faciunt*. The eight 'Salve regina' settings occupy a prominent place among his motets; his *Vater unser im Himmelreich* has survived incomplete. Vaet's secular music comprises seventeen ceremonial motets, including the elegy *Continuo lachrimas* for Clemens non Papa, and three chansons.

95
136

WAELRANT, Hubert (*b* 1516 or 1517; *d* Antwerp, 1595) possibly spent his youth in Italy. (The composer's interest in the genre of the *napolitana* may be an indication of this: in 1565 his collection *Le canzon napolitane* was printed in Venice.) From 1544 he was a tenor at the Church of Our Lady in Antwerp and he was active in the town as a teacher at a music school directed by Gregorius de Coninck. From 1554 Waelrant also made an impact as a music editor; in that year he became associated with the Antwerp printer Jan de Laet, who had already produced a number of editions of the Bible among other works. Together they produced eight collections of motets and four of chansons, Waelrant acting as the editor of the music. The cathedral archives—Antwerp was a diocese from 1559—show that Waelrant checked the tuning of the three new bells in 1563. His name was further linked to the addition of the note si to the hexachord so that the octave could be solmized without mutation.*

Waelrant's sacred music comprises thirty motets and nine psalms. The choice of texts in the motets is striking: his collection of 1556 contains exclusively biblical texts relating to the life of Christ. But his psalms are all based on the metrical translation by Marot. His secular works comprise thirty-four chansons, fifteen madrigals, and forty-eight *napolitane*.

---

* The Spanish theorist Batholomeo Ramos de Pareia, however, had already proposed a new method of solmization in 1482, using eight syllables for the complete octave.

WEERBECKE [Werbeke], Gaspar van (*b* Oudenaarde, *c.*1445; 22
d after 1517) 26

58
went to Italy about 1470 and entered the service of Galeazzo Maria 115
Sforza in Milan. During his first appointment in Milan (from 1472 to 131
1480 or 1481) he acted for a considerable time as 'vice abbate' (director) 145
of the *cantori de camera*. In the same period Josquin, Compère, and 154
Martini were active at the Milanese court as *cantori de capella*. Gaspar made
two journeys to Flanders and Burgundy to recruit singers for Galeazzo.
After the duke's murder many musicians left Milan and, like Josquin,
Gaspar found a new sphere of employment in Rome, where from 1481 to
1489 he was a member of the papal chapel. In 1489 he returned to Milan,
where Galeazzo's brother Lodovico 'il Moro' employed him. (On a visit
to his birthplace he was honoured as 'sanckmeester van den hertoge van
melanen', or singing-master to the Duke of Milan.) Gaspar also had a
special relationship with the court of Philip the Fair; this can be seen
from the fact that his name appears in the lists of the court chapel singers
between 1495 and 1497. He was perhaps back in Milan in the last two
years of the fifteenth century, and after the town was captured by Louis
XII he went again to Rome, where he obtained an appointment in the
papal chapel for the second time. Gasper held prebends from among
other places, the diocese of Utrecht, and in 1515 he was placed on the
waiting-list for prebends in Cambrai and Tournai.

Gaspar's *œuvre* consists almost exclusively of sacred compositions.
Eight Masses by him are known, two Credo settings, three motet cycles
for the Milanese Mass liturgy, twenty-two motets, and a Lamentations
setting. Although he based the *Missa Ave regina coelorum* on chant, he
mainly took secular melodies as his starting-points. One of the motet
cycle, consisting of six motets, was written for Pentecost. Petrucci's first
motet publication (1502) indicates that his motets, which include one
of the earliest settings of the *Stabat mater*, were in demand: no other
composer is represented in the volume by nine pieces. Though some
chansons and the Dutch song *O Venus banth* are attributed to him, probably only the instrumental piece *La Stangetta* is authentic.

WERT, Giaches [Jaches] de (*b* ?Weert, near Antwerp, 1535; 47
d Mantua, 1596) 92

94
was, like Lasso, taken as a young boy to Italy, where he sang as a
choirboy at the court of the Marchioness of Padulla near Naples. His
next appointment took him to the court of Alfonso Gonzaga in

Novellara, near Modena. He was possibly already here in 1553, and in any case stayed until 1558. In 1561 he was recorded as a singer, under Cypriano de Rore, in Parma. Four years later he was appointed *maestro di cappella* to Guglielmo Gonzaga at the ducal chapel of Santa Barbara in Mantua. In this period he made some official journeys to Augsburg and Venice. Wert also regularly visited the court of the d'Este family in Ferrara, and in the 1580s he wrote numerous virtuoso madrigals for the *concerto delle donne*, the famous ensemble of three sopranos. After he was granted Mantuan citizenship in 1580 and Vincenzo Gonzaga had succeeded his father in 1587, Wert also devoted himself to the court theatre. Among other things, he wrote music for the performance of Guarini's *Il pastor fido*.

Wert's liturgical music comprises eight Masses, about 125 hymns, eighteen psalms, five Magnificats, a *St Mark Passion*, and a Te Deum. Because of the strict rules which Guglielmo adopted for the liturgy in the Chapel of Santa Barbara, he based almost all his compositions on chant, with polyphonic sections alternating with the liturgical melodies. In addition, Wert chose texts from the liturgy for his forty-four motets, but here the musical settings are freely composed. For the feast of the patron saint of the Mantuan chapel he wrote the six-part motet *Beata Barbara*. His secular pieces, about 200 in all, belong for the most part to the genre of the madrigal. Over a half are composed on texts of high literary value, by Petrarch, Ariosto, Tasso, and Guarini among others. But there are also many *villanelle* and *moresche*, which, like some of the madrigals, were used for stage productions. Finally, one might mention Wert's four instrumental fantasies.

20 WILLAERT [Villard, Vuigliart], Adrian [Adriano Fiammingo]
27 (*b* ?Roeselare, *c*.1485; *d* Venice, 1562)
36
46 According to his pupil Gioseffo Zarlino he studied law in Paris and there
68 came into contact with the French court composer Jean Mouton, from
92 whom he received his musical education. In 1515 he entered the service
93 of Cardinal Ippolito I d'Este, and worked in both Rome and Ferrara.
95 Two years later Willaert went with the cardinal to Hungary (Ippolito
104 was Archbishop of Esztergom). In 1519 the composer returned to
105 Ferrara, and after Ippolito's death in 1520 he accepted an appointment
114 from Duke Alfonso d'Este. When the post of *maestro di cappella* at St
115 Mark's in Venice became vacant in 1527, Willaert was appointed; he
124
126 occupied this excellently paid post for thirty-five years, interrupting his

FIG. 50. Portrait of Adrian Willaert. Woodcut in his *Musica nova*, printed by Antonio Gardano in Venice in 1559.

133 stay on only two occasions for journeys to Flanders. Cypriano de Rore,
136 Jakob Buus, and many Italian composers were among his pupils.

139   Willaert's liturgical music consists of eight or nine Masses, thirty
161 hymns, twenty-six psalms, and two Magnificat settings. In almost all his
167 Masses he parodies a motet, showing a preference for those of Mouton.
174 Some of his Masses, including *Gaude Barbara*, are preserved in choirbooks in 's-Hertogenbosch. Among his psalms there are six compositions for two choirs, which he wrote jointly with Jachet of Mantua. His
corpus of motets, comprising over 170 pieces, may be considered extensive; it includes works on liturgical texts besides settings of the Mass
Propers and also many paraliturgical works. His secular works on Latin
texts contain a number of ceremonial motets and two settings of 'Dulces
exuviae' from Virgil's *Aeneid*. There are fifty-six madrigals on Italian
texts, including twenty-five on poems by Petrarch and twenty-two *villanelle*. Among his sixty chansons a number of texts appear in several
settings, such as the versions of *Petite camusette* for four and six voices.
Finally, at least twelve instrumental ricercars have been preserved.

GLOSSARY

Acrostic — Poem in which the first letters of the lines together form a word, often the name of person.

Alleluia — Chant in the Mass Proper which follows the GRADUAL.

Alternatim — See p. 31.

Antiphon — Liturgical verse which is sung before and after a psalm.

Ars subtilior — The style of the late-fourteenth-century ballades, distinguished by florid melodies and refined rhythms (see BALLADE).

Ballade — An important form in French secular music of the fourteenth century which was also used in the fifteenth. The text normally consists of three strophes, each of which ends with the same line of text (refrain) and are sung to the same music. The musical form follows the scheme ababcD, where D is the refrain. The song is for one to three parts, vocal or instrumental.

Ballata — Originally a dance song; the most important form in Italian secular music of the fourteenth century. The form is like that of the French VIRELAI. The scoring is generally for voices and instruments (see p. 89).

Basse danse — A French court dance of the fifteenth and sixteenth centuries. The name refers to the steps, which are performed close to the ground, in contrast with the jumping-dance.

Bicinium — A name used in the sixteenth century for a two-part vocal or instrumental composition.

Block chords — A set of chords, usually in three parts, each lasting a few beats.

Breve	A note-value equal to a half or third of a longa, depending on the mensuration sign.
Breviary	Book of hours or prayers.
Caccia	Hunting song; a form of Italian fourteenth-century secular music. The parts are canonic and often include imitations of hunting-calls.
Canción	A Spanish song.
Canon	A polyphonic composition using a strict imitative technique: the first part is exactly repeated by one or more other parts starting at a later point.
Cantus firmus	Literally: firm song. The cantus firmus is a chant which functions as the basis for a polyphonic composition and as such is recognizable from the large note-values in which it is notated.
Cantus prius factus (c.p.f.)	See p. 27.
Canzona	A form of instrumental music of the sixteenth and seventeenth centuries which developed from the chanson.
Canzone	A song on an Italian text; in the sixteenth century it generally had a popular character.
Chromatic	A succession of semitones, such as the motif B–C–C#–D–D#–E ... in Rore's motet *Calami sonum*. Chromatic is the opposite of DIATONIC.
Circle of fifths	The circular, clockwise arrangement of the tonics of the twelve keys in a series of rising fifths, whereby a sharp is added to the tonality each time. If the pattern is followed in the opposite direction, the notes appear as a series of falling fifths, whereby a flat is added each time. The circle of fifths is closed only in the system of equal temperament.
Circulatio	Melodic figure with a circular shape.
Color	See p. 34.
Communion	Chant in the Mass Proper which is performed during the Communion.

Consecration	See EUCHARIST.
Counterpoint	Literally: note against note (*punctus contra punctum*). This term means the art of writing one or more melodies against an existing melody. In invertible counterpoint the parts are composed in such a way that they can be exchanged with each other, for example in octaves (see OCTAVE). This form of counterpoint was described for the first time in the sixteenth century. According to Kiesewetter (see p. 1) invertible counterpoint consisted of complex canonic structures which had been developed by Johannes Ockeghem (see CANON).
Diatonic	A succession of stepwise notes, such as C–D–E–F–G–A–B–C. Diatonic is the opposite of CHROMATIC.
Discant song	A song in which the sung text lies in the upper voice.
Doxology	An expression of praise, for example as the closing formula of a psalm.
Eucharist	The giving of thanks and praise over the gifts of bread and wine during the celebration of Mass.
Fermata	A sign above a note indicating that its duration must be lengthened by an unspecified duration.
Ficta	See MUSICA FICTA.
Fifth	Interval of five notes.
Fourth	Interval of four notes.
Frottola	The most important form in Italian secular music of the second half of the fifteenth century. The text, not normally of the highest literary quality, is presented in the upper voice, and the three lower parts are generally instrumental. The structure of the song depends on the form of the poem used.
Gradual	Chant in the Mass Proper which follows the reading of the epistle.

Harmony	Generally the name for a chord, but more particularly for a consonant chord.
Hexachord	Row of six notes which form part of the system developed by Guido d'Arezzo in the eleventh century. The six notes were always called ut, re, mi, fa, sol, and la, whatever pitch the row was applied to. The hexachord which begins on C (C–D–E–F–G–A) was called *naturale*, that on F (F–G–A–Bb–C–D) the *molle* and that on G (G–A–B–C–D–E) the *durum*. The semitone lies between the third and fourth notes. By means of a 'mutation', one can move from one hexachord to another.
Homophony	Literally: sounding at the same time. Homophony is the opposite of POLYPHONY and means that the different parts of a composition are written in the same rhythm, the melodic voice leading the others.
Imitation technique	See p 28.
Incipit	The beginning or the first notes of a composition.
Introit	Chant in the Mass Proper which is performed as the priest enters; it precedes the Kyrie.
Isoperiodic	See p. 32.
Jubilus	A melodic phrase on a single vowel at the end of a chant.
Kyriale	Liturgical book containing only the chants of the Ordinary of the Mass (beginning with the Kyrie).
Lamentations	The Lamentations of Jeremiah in the Holy Week liturgy.
Longa	A note-value; the length is two or three times the value of the BREVE, depending on the mensuration sign.
Madrigal	Name for two different forms of secular vocal music on Italian texts in the fourteenth and sixteenth centuries respectively. Little can be said

with certainty about the derivation of the word. The fourteenth-century madrigal consists of two or three strophes which are sung to the same music, and ends with a ritornello with different music. It is generally in two parts. The sixteenth-century madrigal is through-composed and generally uses four to six vocal parts (see pp. 92–5).

Magnificat	Mary's song of praise (Luke 1: 46–55); it had already appeared in the Roman liturgy before the time of Pope Gregory I (*c*.540–602), and was frequently set to polyphony from the fifteenth century onwards.
Melisma	An expressive vocal passage sung to a single syllable.
Mensuration	Term from the so-called mensurally notated music of the thirteenth to sixteenth centuries, in which each note had a fixed value dependent on the mensuration sign or proportion signs used; these indicated the diminution or expansion of the normal note-values according to mathematical ratios.
Migrans	See p. 29.
Mode	Row of eight notes which determines the character of the melody and harmony according to the position of the two semitones. In medieval music eight modes were in use: Dorian and Hypodorian (beginning on D and A respectively), Phrygian and Hypophrygian (beginning on E and B), Lydian and Hypolydian (beginning on F and C), Mixolydian and Hypomixolydian (beginning on G and D). In the sixteenth century the number of modes was enlarged to twelve by the addition of the Ionian (C and G) and Aeolian (A and E).
Moresca	A pantomime dance from the sixteenth century (see p. 95).

Motet	Originally a form of early polyphonic music, which underwent great changes in the course of the centuries. While the fourteenth-century motet had different French and Latin texts in the various parts, the fifteenth- and sixteenth-century motet generally had only one text, invariably in Latin. As Latin came to be chosen as the only language for the text, the motet developed a more religious character (see pp. 3 and 23).
Musica ficta	In the narrowest sense of the term, unnotated, but nevertheless important accidentals applied to particular notes in polyphonic music before 1600. In modern editions of this music such sharps and flats are indicated above rather than in front of the notes concerned.
Napolitana	See p. 95.
Octave	Interval of eight notes.
Offertory	Chant in the Mass Proper which is sung during the offering of the bread and wine.
Office	The communal prayer of the liturgy which is celebrated eight times a day, and comprises psalms, antiphons, responsories, and hymns among other things. The office is built around the Mass, the focus of worship.
Oltremontani	An expression used in Italy to refer to persons who came 'from the other side of the mountains' (i.e. the Alps).
Ordinary	The 'unchanging' chants of the Mass, namely Kyrie, Gloria, Credo, Sanctus, and Agnus Dei.
Organum	Name for the earliest form of improvised polyphonic music, which was used in Western Europe from the ninth century, and was adopted as a compositional form in the twelfth century (see POLYPHONY).
Paraphrase	See p. 30.
Parody	See p. 46.

Passion	A musical setting of the story of Christ's sufferings according to one of the four evangelists. During the fifteenth and sixteenth centuries there were two types: the so-called responsorial Passion, in which the part of the evangelist was sung by a solo voice (possibly in chant), and the other parts in polyphony; and the motet Passion, in which the whole text was set polyphonically.
Picture motet	See p. 74.
Polyphony	Literally: mulit-sounding. Polyphony is the opposite of HOMOPHONY and means that the various parts of a composition are independent from each other with regard to melody and rhythm (see also COUNTERPOINT).
Prebend	Income from church property awarded to a cleric as payment for duties performed.
Preces	Generally, prayers, but in particular the prayers of petition in the OFFICE.
Preface	Chant sung by a priest before the Sanctus in the Mass.
Prolatio major	The division of the semibreve into three minims.
Prolatio minor	The division of the semibreve into two minims.
Proper	The 'changing' parts of the Mass, namely Introit, Gradual, Alleluia, Tract, Offertory, and Communion. Individual days of the Church year thus have their own chants.
Proportion canon	CANON in which the various parts are identical in melodic line but differ in rhythm. The parts of such a canon each have their own mensuration sign, which defines the note-values for the part independently of the others.
Psalmody	The monophonic presentation of psalms whereby verses or parts of verses are sung alternately by two choirs, or by soloist and choir.
Quadrivium	See p. 127.

Quodlibet	A composition in which well-known melodies (and texts) are combined with each other in a humorous manner.
Recto tono	At a constant pitch.
Remissio peccatorum	The forgiveness of sins.
Responsory	A chant form whereby solo passages alternate with answers from the choir. In sixteenth-century music responsories are also set as motets: the respond forms the first part, and the solo section and the repeated section (second half) of the respond the second part of the motet (ABCB).
Ricercar	A composition with a polyphonic, imitative structure (see pp.115 ff.).
Rondeau	The most important form of fifteenth-century French secular music. The musical setting of the refrain, the opening of the poem, is also used for the strophes which follow. The refrain recurs after each strophe, possibly in a shortened form. The scoring is normally for voices and instruments.
Rota	Medieval rondo form.
Sequence	The repetition of a set group of notes at a higher or lower pitch.
Sequentia	A Latin medieval liturgical chant based on a poem in which the verses form rhyming pairs.
Sixth	Interval of six notes.
Soggetto cavato	See p. 37.
Soggetto ostinato	See p. 36.
Superius	The highest voice of a polyphonic composition.
Talea	See p. 34.
Tempus imperfectum	The division of the BREVE into two semibreves.
Tempus perfectum	The division of the BREVE into three semibreves.
Third	Interval of three notes.
Toccata	See p. 124.
Tone	Another word for MODE.

Tract	Chant in the Mass Proper that replaces the ALLELUIA from Septuagesima to Easter.
Transposition	The performance of a melody or entire composition at a different pitch.
Trinitas in unitate	Literally: Trinity in unity. This motto was sometimes written on three-part canons to indicate that a single notated part could yield two others.
Trope	See p. 21.
Unison	The 'interval' between two notes of the same pitch.
Varietas	The striving in Renaissance art after continuous change and alternation; the absence of monotony.
Villanella	See p. 95.
Virelai	A form in fourteenth-century French poetry and music which was used occasionally in the fifteenth. Its structure is similar to that of the Italian BALLATA, but the lengths of the refrain and the strophe (or two strophes) are less regular. The scoring is usually for voices and instruments.